My Cousin Maria Schneider

A MEMOIR

Vanessa Schneider

Translated by Molly Ringwald

Scribner

NEW YORK   LONDON   TORONTO   SYDNEY   NEW DELHI

Scribner
An Imprint of Simon & Schuster, LLC
1230 Avenue of the Americas
New York, NY 10020

This Scribner trade paperback edition April 2024

SCRIBNER and design are trademarks of Simon & Schuster, LLC

Simon & Schuster: Celebrating 100 Years of Publishing in 2024

For information about special discounts for bulk purchases,
please contact Simon & Schuster Special Sales
at 1-866-506-1949 or business@simonandschuster.com.

The Simon & Schuster Speakers Bureau can bring authors to your live event.
For more information, or to book an event, contact the
Simon & Schuster Speakers Bureau at 1-866-248-3049 or
visit our website at www.simonspeakers.com.

Interior design by Ruth Lee-Mui

Manufactured in the United States of America

1   3   5   7   9   10   8   6   4   2

Library of Congress Cataloging-in-Publication Data has been applied for.

ISBN 978-1-9821-4150-9
ISBN 978-1-9821-4153-0 (pbk)
ISBN 978-1-9821-4154-7 (ebook)

My Cousin
Maria Schneider

"I had a beautiful life," you say with a tired smile. It's a few days before your death and you're lost in happy memories. Your voice is soft, like a finger gliding along a piece of velvet. You don't say it to make us happy, or to convince yourself—that isn't your way.

At first, I don't understand. Your declaration seems like a dissonant note in an otherwise harmonic chord. For so long now I've been worrying about you—years of my life spent living through your pain and misfortune until it became nearly indistinguishable from my own. And yet, here we are.

"I had a beautiful life."

I'm so glad you see it this way.

You are fifty-eight years old when you die. Far too young—and yet we never thought you would make it even that long. Most people assumed that you had died years ago. To them, you're already a figure from the distant past.

After your death, the media thrusts you back into the spotlight. The articles all tell the same story, more or less, cobbled together from the same hackneyed clichés: "Erotic Actress" and "Lost Child of the Cinema." They write about *The Last Tango in Paris* and of your "ruined career" and "tragic destiny." There's the hedonism of the seventies, the cruelty of the film business and, of course, the sex and drugs.

No one writes about how, when you die, you are sipping champagne, your favorite drink—the one that could make you forget your childhood and help fill in the cracks of a fractured, sensitive soul. You leave us amidst bubbles and bursts of laughter, loving faces and smiles—upright with your head held high, a little tipsy. With panache.

L'Église Saint-Roch, known as the church of artists and film stars, is located in the heart of Paris, the city you tried and failed so many times to leave. It's in this particular church that you wanted us to say our goodbyes to you. You planned the ceremony with stunning precision, down to the music that would be played—mostly Bach—and the people who were to be invited. With age you'd become a believer again, rediscovering all the religious rituals from your childhood. You started lighting candles in church when you came for prayer, while continuing to espouse the veracity of your other preoccupation, astrology—the influence of the positions of planets on people. The incongruity of these beliefs never seemed to bother you.

On the day of your funeral, it's pouring rain, and water streams down the bell tower of the Church of Saint Roch. Alain Delon is seated in the first row. I'm not sure when you had seen him last, but here he is, with his mane of white hair and dark eyebrows, seated in the pew reserved for family. He had insisted on giving the first eulogy. Soberly, he reads aloud the letter Brigitte Bardot wrote for you but didn't have the strength to come read herself, and his deep voice echoes throughout the church. He inhabits the words as if they're his own. Delon and Bardot, your "film godparents," had both wanted to say the same thing anyway.

There are many people gathered that day under the church's cold vaulted ceiling; your friends, the remainder of our broken family, one or two ministers of culture, and complete strangers who have come to pay their respects. Your father's family, the Gélins, and your half sisters and brothers meet later at the Père Lachaise cemetery, part of an intimate group that will gather for your cremation. There are faces I struggle to put a name to, film icons from the seventies and survivors of the film industry like you—Dominique Sanda and Christine Boisson, star of the film *Emmanuelle*, are both there. They have such admiration for you, and so many fond memories—I wish you could've seen it.

Your mother is absent. She elected not to take the trip from Nice to Paris, saying she was too tired.

I keep everything in a red plastic folder, the kind with the two rubber bands angled at the corners to keep it closed. Inside are photos of you torn from magazines, with interviews and press clippings from your films. I'm in elementary school, and I collect everything ever written about you with a perseverance that borders on obsession. I carefully cut out each article in which your name appears using those little safety scissors with the rounded ends. I beg my mother to entrust me with the pictures of you at my age, along with your first drawings, and I decorate the folder containing my treasures with star-shaped stickers and rainbow glitter. On the front of the folder I glue a black-and-white photo of you from a newspaper that was printed on poor-quality paper. In the picture your cheeks are round, and you wear the radiant smile I saw so rarely in person. I cover the picture with Scotch tape to safeguard it from age, and in what was probably my childish attempt to protect you from life's contamination.

Over the years, as the file grows, I notice with disappointment that each piece I collect has less to do with your films and more with the turbulence of your personal life. The features and reviews are replaced by tabloid stories with salacious headlines. As I get older, even these articles begin to disappear, and there's rarely anything new to put in the red folder. Occasionally, you appear in the kind of low-budget international film that's sure never to be released in France, but you're no longer considered for the lead roles, and after a while you cease to interest even the journalists. Like so many others of your generation, you join the troop of discarded stars, beaten down and rejected by a new era that has no place for rebels. You're no longer my childhood celebrity, the one strangers recognize on the street with a frisson of excitement and envy, but you remain my special cousin for whom I harbor a tender and morbid fascination. A precious, broken family jewel, hidden away in a secret drawer.

Throughout my adolescence, I keep track of the red folder—the testament to your former glory. I take it with me everywhere, reading and rereading the fragments of your life. I don't always recognize the girl in the stories the press chooses to tell. They are half-truths, approximations, fantasies, and some blatant falsehoods. But even so, there is usually some element of truth. A young girl ravaged by an explosive public debut. The weight of a terrible childhood too heavy to carry. In the end, yours is a path that the women in our family tend to follow, a trajectory that our cousins and I could have easily taken had you not, in some way, been sacrificed for us.

When I'm a child, on the rare occasions I open the red folder in front of friends, I receive looks of bewilderment and suspicion. Who is this actress who is supposed to have been so successful, but who no one's ever heard of? I'm suspected of lying, of inventing a famous relative to get attention. When I move out of my parents' apartment at twenty years old, I decide to leave the folder at the family house in the country to keep it from getting lost during the itinerant years of young adulthood.

The old farmhouse is a repository of memories. In a room that's ostensibly my father's office (although I never saw him work there), he keeps hundreds of papers tracing his revolutionary ambitions as well as the archives from the extreme Left Maoist political organization to which he once belonged. There's also a collection of drawings, some by you, thrown together in colorful disarray alongside stacks of the very first issues of *Libération*, the left-wing newspaper founded in 1973 by Jean-Paul Sartre and Serge July, for which I would later work as a journalist. The farmhouse suits you: wallpaper with big orange and chartreuse flowers, patched furniture and salvaged objects, a sprawling, overgrown garden that during my childhood was regularly transformed into a hippie haven, a place where men and women dressed in tunics gathered around a campfire and strummed guitars while smoking enormous joints. It seems the perfect place to keep the folder safe.

Every time I come to visit the house in the country, I take the red folder out of the drawer and examine its contents. As the years pass, the smell of dust grows stronger. The photos fade and the paper begins to erode from the humidity. One day I can't find the folder at all. It seems to have vanished entirely. I'm heartbroken. I can't shake the feeling that the folder somehow represents you: the pride and embarrassment it brought me, its comforting omnipresence, until its gradual, eventual disappearance. Now that the folder is gone, I know that one day, I will have to tell your story.

In my earliest photo of you, you're about twelve years old. My mother is behind the camera, and you're posing with my father—your uncle—who is only a few years older than you and who, at twenty, appears so young to me now. In the black-and-white snapshot, the two of you look like sad children. You're leaning against a tree staring at the lens with the wide eyes of a frightened fawn. Your hair is shorn like a boy's—your mother had recently and brutally decided to chop it off. Perhaps you had become too beautiful for her taste. The way you hold your head hints at the determined young woman you are soon to become, but you still have a young girl's silhouette, and you seem unsure of yourself. You wear the worried expression of a child who senses her path in life will be paved with sharp and jagged stones.

You are born just after World War II, during European reconstruction, at the beginning of the postwar boom. That same year, a strange machine manufactured by IBM—the first commercial scientific computer—is released in the United States. In France, our homes are still heated with coal and our laundry is done by hand. Children don't receive gifts except on Christmas and birthdays. Families do not travel, or have refrigerators. Two thirds of the population don't even have running water, and only the very wealthy own televisions. The schools are segregated by gender so that the girls grow up together away from the gaze of boys. They play with jacks and yo-yos, and can't wait until they're old enough for sleepovers. The birth control pill doesn't exist. Couples do their best to avoid unwanted pregnancies by using the rhythm method and, when that fails, secret illegal abortions. Former Resistance fighter and Catholic priest Abbé Pierre founds the Emmaus movement to bring financial aid to those most in need.

You're considered a peacetime child, and yet the wars are certainly not finished. Decolonization is bloody, first in Indochina (now Vietnam) and then in Algeria. A new world map is being drawn. Stalin dies in March 1953, and Elizabeth is crowned

queen of England a few months later. In France, the command-
ing presence of Charles de Gaulle rules politics. On the fourth
of November 1956, Soviet tanks enter Budapest and wipe out
the Hungarian insurrection. Europe, and soon the world, is cut
in half—vast swaths of battleground between the pro- and anti-
communists. The wars become colder by the day.

Others describe you as a happy and playful child, but to your
mother you are intolerable, particularly in comparison to her
two sons, whom she openly adores. She never hid the identity
of your father from you. Daniel Gélin, the great French actor,
was unable to give you his name because you were born out of
wedlock and the law at the time forbade him from legally recognizing you. In Melun, where you spent your early years, he
would come to see you on occasion, but so rarely you kept no
memory of him. Eventually the visits stopped altogether. Your
mother tells you this is your fault—that he's angry with you, that
he doesn't love you or want to see you. In fact, it's she who wants
to keep you at a distance.

Eventually your mother insists she can't take it anymore; she
can barely take care of herself, let alone you. She wants to send
you away to be looked after by a nursemaid. A professional will
know what to do, she says: she'll teach you rules, give you an education, keep you on track. You're still so young, only eight years
old, when your mother informs you that she's found someone.
I imagine you at first responding to the news in silence, your
anguish restrained by rage and terror. You don't want to go. You
don't want to leave your mother and brothers. Eventually you
cry, and scream, but no one listens to you. Your mother leaves

you with a stranger for two years, during which time you hear not one word from her.

You are just shy of ten years old when you are returned to your family.

Your mother's sex life was never a secret to you, just as her mother's was not to her. Our family hides nothing. A story often told in our home, always with an air of disapproval, is of the time your mother was in bed with a man and called out for you to fetch her diaphragm. She demanded it in the same curt, imperious tone she always used with you, making it clear you had no choice but to comply. You looked for it in the bathroom, rummaging around with shaking hands, finally managing to locate it in the cabinet under the sink. She told you countless times not to drop it, that it's extremely fragile and cost a fortune. You walked so slowly to her bedroom, holding it carefully in your hands, that she shouted for you to hurry up. You safely delivered the diaphragm and ran back to your room.

And now you are fourteen and your beauty grows more evident with each passing day. Your face metamorphoses into that of a young woman. The bend in your nose straightens out, your skin becomes smooth, your eyes suddenly seem a little too big for your face. Your stomach and breasts bloat every month as your body prepares for menstruation. You try to disguise the changes under oversize sweaters, but no matter how much you hide, the boys notice you. Their looks linger on the curves of your figure. Grown men turn around to ogle you as you pass in the street. Your mother questions you incessantly, and one day you give in and admit to having a sweetheart. In response to this news there's only one thing that interests her.

"Did you sleep with him?" she asks. The question hurts and offends you—how could she think such a thing?

"No, of course not! I wouldn't do that!" you insist.

She sucks her teeth and rolls her eyes. "My poor girl. What a coward you are!"

You're fifteen years old, the age your mother was when she had her first child and the age our grandmother was when she was forced to marry. In our family, it's the age at which young women are brutally thrown into adulthood, when mothers cease to protect their daughters. Yours kicks you out after a terrible argument at your home. There are whispers that your mother caught your stepfather in your bed. Papa and Maman suggest that you come to live with them in a tiny one-bedroom apartment on the Avenue de la Grande Armée, a street that forms the boundary between the 16th and 17th arrondissements of Paris.

You adore my parents, and you're enamored with their bohemian lifestyle. At last, you feel free. You attend high school at the Lycée Racine and are a good student. It's 1967 and I'm not born yet. My father is still a college student, and my mother works as a book editor at Maspero publishing house in the Latin Quarter. She hangs out with the *Cahiers du Cinéma* gang and spends her free time going to see films at the Cinémathèque Française, the French museum of film. Papa studies politics, the economy, and the law. He moves in the most radical left-wing circles, the ones that are ready to take up arms in the name of revolution. He reads the newspapers and organizes protests, slipping away to meetings during the day with the air of a conspirator and returning home in the evening with a euphoric smile. Having heard nothing of politics up until that point in your life, you find it all novel and amusing. In this milieu of the mid-sixties, you call yourself a Gaullist. You aren't sure exactly what it means but you call yourself one anyway.

My parents don't believe in God. Jesus and the Virgin Mary have been replaced in their cosmology by Freud and Mao. After moving in with them you discover that something called "psychoanalysis" exists. It amuses you about as much as the revolution, and you dismiss it as just another of my father's eccentricities. Anyway, it's the cinema that really intrigues you. You ask my parents to tell you about the newest films and then run to the theaters to discover them for yourself. Maman recommends you to a young director friend of hers who is casting his film. He's looking for someone resembling the girl in Robert Bresson's 1967 film *Mouchette*, someone young with a dark, sullen manner, and he arranges for you to film a screen test but ultimately finds you too timid. Maman is disappointed, arguing that, on the contrary, you possess a wild intensity that's completely innate. She's unable to convince him to give you the part but manages to persuade him to give you the reel from your screen test. I have no idea if you kept it.

You are barely sixteen years old when one day you return home with your cheeks on fire. You have something extraordinary to share with my parents. "You'll never guess what I did today!" You're so deliriously excited anticipating their reaction that the words come out all jumbled. That afternoon, on impulse, you went to your father's apartment and rang the bell. You hadn't seen him for years but were very well received! He and Danièle Delorme had divorced and after a brief affair with Ursula Andress, he settled down with the former Dior model Sylvie Hirsch, with whom he had two other children, Manuel and Fiona. He told you to come back whenever you liked. Really, whenever!

Soon you stop going to school and go everywhere with him instead. You join him on set, where he introduces you as his daughter. He's proud of you. You're beautiful, have artistic talent, and are curious about so many things. He too makes you swell with pride. A dark and handsome leading man with a career that's the envy of film actors on both sides of the Atlantic. He's acted for many of the greats, from Sacha Guitry and Jean Cocteau to Alfred Hitchcock.

At the end of each day, you return home breathless and recount everything you saw. In the bubble of the film set you are adored. People show interest in you, and you relish it. You talk to my parents nonstop about the camera and lights, the tangle of cords and the intricate ballet of the film technicians behind the camera—the multiple takes, scenes repeated over and over. When you come home you draw everything you've seen with your pastels as if trying to remember the fragments of a dream.

Gélin brings you to the set but also to clubs and parties, introducing you to the nightlife of Paris. In Montparnasse, where he's counted among its most famous residents, it's rumored that he's a libertine leading a life of debauchery behind the façade of a well-behaved married man. He's known for doing drugs and seducing women and men alike. Even though you're his daughter, and still so young, he drags you from place to place until dawn as though you're his latest conquest.

One night you're with him in the wee hours at Chez Castel— the Parisian hot spot of the moment. It's six in the morning and the nightclub is closing, but he's not ready to let go of you yet. He decides, at that moment, it's absolutely urgent that he introduce you to your sister and brother, and he brings you back to his apartment. "Fiona, Fiona!" he calls out to your sleeping six-year-old half sister. He shakes her awake. "Fiona, this is your sister, Maria." She opens her eyes. You smile at her, a little embarrassed. She blinks at you, not sure if she's awake or dreaming.

Suddenly your father is tired and wants to go to bed. "See you later," he mumbles, half asleep as he slides a few francs into your hand for the taxi. You return to my parents' apartment exhausted but wired, your clothes and hair reeking of cigarettes and alcohol. You replay the evening over and over in your mind. The images and the faces scramble. You already know you won't be going to school when you wake up.

A few days later your father calls you. "Are you ready? I'll pick you up in ten minutes." You get dressed, quickly line your eyes in kohl, and run outside to meet him. He drives you to more places and more parties where you meet people you've seen only in the pages of magazines. You go everywhere with your father, whom you still call "Monsieur."

You are sixteen years old and it's time to move again. Maman has told you that you can't stay with her and your uncle any longer, explaining that she's pregnant and will soon be having a baby. I'm that baby. The apartment has only one bedroom and it's far too small for four. She tells you that you can take your time, that there's no rush, she just wants to give you advance warning to find another solution. My arrival equals your departure—that's the story I will always be told. Every time I hear it, I have the unpleasant sensation of having chased you away—that had you stayed with Papa and Maman, perhaps your life would have unfolded differently.

You are eighteen years old and you dance. You're no longer the timid little girl, or the shy adolescent. You dance anywhere you find yourself—on the tables of nightclubs in Corsica, at Chez Castel in Paris. You dance all night, to Jimi Hendrix, Janis Joplin, Jim Morrison, the Velvet Underground. You dance and dream of America. You dance with no thought of what you're going to do tomorrow. You dress in miniskirts and vintage leather jackets, your wrists covered in stacks of bracelets.

You dance and drink and dance and smoke. You dance and kiss boys, you dance and kiss girls. You hang out at the hot spots of Montparnasse, Le Select or La Coupole. You're spotted one night with the actress Bulle Ogier, and then the next with Catherine Deneuve. The child model Eva Ionesco, who's even younger than you, will later recall spotting you at a table with Jean-Pierre Léaud. Your "sensual abandon" will be forever etched in her memory, as she will recount in her memoir. A heavily made-up woman tells Ionesco that you are Brigitte Bardot's protégée—one of her "amazons." You enter the seventies with a flourish and are received with open arms.

Fourteen months after my birth, my little brother is born and we move into a bigger apartment. We now live in low-income housing in the 13th arrondissement, and you come to visit us. You're nineteen years old and you hang out with my parents and their circle of friends, the "grown-ups"; the kids don't interest you much. People come and go from the apartment all the time: psychoanalysts, artists, workers, militants planning the revolution with my father, South Americans escaping the fascist dictatorships of their homeland. The apartment is warm and colorful. The walls are covered in Indian textiles, the furniture a mix of baroque pieces salvaged from the street and Scandinavian furniture purchased from the discount store. You love to come over. There's always something to eat and drink and smoke. It's a poetic and hazy world.

I was named Vanessa after Vanessa Redgrave, whom my parents had seen in *Blow-Up*, by Michelangelo Antonioni. They had to convince the civil court officer to register me since the name isn't in the calendar of the saints, as most French names are.

Home is both the low-income housing and Bayreuth, where my parents bring us every summer for the opera festival. Maria Callas and Bob Dylan alternate on the record player. I'm not exactly sure *what* we are, if we are black or white, rich or poor, bourgeois or working class. I know that my family is educated, intellectual, and academic. The branches of our family tree have grown in many different directions. We have leading doctors, political figures, and former ministers, but I'm told that none of this matters because the social classes are in the process of being abolished, and that being a worker is worth much more than simply being a student. I don't understand much of anything. However, I do recognize that my parents are different from the parents of my classmates. My mother's skin is dark. She wears her hair in an Afro that frames her beautiful face, and my father's hair skims his shoulders. While my friends go to summer camps, my family goes to the mountains in rugged Cévennes. Other families do the catechism, but ours believe in neither God nor Santa Claus—even less the Easter Bunny. My mother believes that children should not be lied to. We own a television but only to watch political programs. The rooms are overrun with books. All of the dishes are washed by hand, the coffee is ground with a mill, and we make our own yogurt and ice cream. My brother and I are forbidden to eat candy or drink soda—everything that comes from America is forbidden, starting with Coca-Cola (the symbol of imperialism), but occasionally we have lunch at the Casino Cafétéria, where all the rules are forgotten for a special treat.

A huge tapestry of Karl Marx hangs on the wall of our living room. His expression is stern, but the fabric upon which his portrait is embroidered is soft and silky. As soon as I'm big enough, I hoist myself up onto a little purple plastic stool to pet him.

My father's work seems so serious to me. The protests and strikes are fomented in a cloud of smoke, amidst a clamor of earnest solemnity. At the moment he's a senior official in the Ministry of Finance. I know that my father, with his long shaggy hair, doesn't resemble his work colleagues any more than he does my friends' fathers, but I find both of my parents to be the epitome of beauty and even more so you, when you arrive with your flea market outfits and fringed shoulder bags. You're magnificent, young and free. I feel privileged to be in your orbit, to lounge in your arms and listen to you speak words and talk about concepts that I've not yet mastered.

All of this was before I understood what kind of family we were, before the shame arrived.

You are almost eighteen years old and Alain Delon loves you like a little sister. It was your father who introduced you. You dream of making movies and Delon brings you to the set with him, introducing you to everyone by your first name. No one dares to question your presence. You glide in his wake, observing his manner and gestures. You study the intensity of his acting and absorb his brute charisma. People think of him as hard, and maybe a little mean, but he's gentle with you. He tells you that he'll help you find parts, and indeed he gets you hired on the 1970 Roger Kahane film *The Love Mates*. It's the story of a menage à trois in which Mireille Darc (Delon's girlfriend at the time) plays the role of the betrayed wife. The script was inspired by the couple's real-life relationship with Maddly Bamy, the gorgeous Guadeloupean actress who later became the life partner of Jacques Brel.

This brief film appearance gets you attention in the press, where, presumably for reasons of efficiency, the magazine renames you Maria Gelin. In a photo taken on the set, Delon holds you in his arms in a gesture that's both tender and protective. His hair is longer than usual. He's wearing a white shirt over faded black jeans that are a little flared above square-toed moccasins, with a cashmere sweater knotted over his shoulders. Your idiosyncratic way of dressing contrasts with his more staid appearance. You're a young woman very much of your time, wearing a light suede microminiskirt with a large studded belt slung low on your hips. A striped wool satchel hangs from your shoulder. Tall, fitted boots accentuate the shape of your legs. You're both leaning against an iron railing over a stream, with an old stone wall covered in vines behind you. At the moment the photo was taken, the two of you are laughing. Delon has been a movie star for a while now but is still breathtakingly beautiful. Next to him, you have the victorious smile of an unloved child getting revenge on life. Everything's in front of you and all the film greats are predicting a brilliant future. The film doesn't do well, but you couldn't care less. For the first time you see your name in the credits of a movie.

Bardot's letter, as read by Delon during your funeral in the Saint Roch church, is both awkward and touching. "With her eternal woman-child face and personality of a wild cat, she conquered the world with the brilliance of a flaming meteorite pulverizing everything in its way. A bright but ephemeral life in which, by offering her velvety body to Marlon Brando at the height of her fame, she shocked and scandalized the world with her lack of inhibition, forever changing it with her insolence, and personifying an era. Yet hidden underneath the boldness was a lost heart, a little girl who, drifting with no home port, propelled higher and higher without preparation, inevitably falling without a parachute and delivered to all manner of excesses to fill the emptiness left by the fame that had abandoned her."

You and Brigitte Bardot were destined to meet. She had known your mother while she was pregnant with you, and your father and his first wife, Danièle Delorme, were the witnesses for her first marriage, to Roger Vadim. Bardot was eighteen years old on her wedding day, in a time when most women in France didn't marry until the age of twenty-one. After a suicide attempt in which she put her head into a gas oven, her father had signed a waiver giving his consent for her to marry.

In 1969, the year I was born, you play a small part in *Women*, a film by Jean Aurel, starring Bardot. She spots you at the

Boulogne-Billancourt studio, probably recognizing herself in your fierce kitten-like features. She talks to you and you respond naturally. No one makes you starstruck, not even one of the biggest sex symbols of the twentieth century. You mention that you're looking for somewhere to live and without a second thought she gives you her address. The following evening, dressed in a white blouse with jeans and sneakers, you arrive at Bardot's apartment—71 Avenue Paul-Doumer in the 16th arrondissement of Paris.

So many years later, in the center of the Saint Roch church, you're resting in a small coffin. My uncle George is giving his eulogy. He says only what you would've liked to hear, and avoids anything that would have upset you. In his tender tribute, my uncle says that he prefers to remember you with the wind in your hair, laughing until you cried in a convertible driven by Jack Nicholson, with whom you shared the screen in Antonioni's *The Passenger*. He will not speak about the film that both brought you fame and cursed you. *The Last Tango in Paris* will not be mentioned at your funeral.

For decades you refused to speak about *Tango*. Anytime the movie was mentioned, you froze. In an interview in 1983, more than ten years after the film was released, you implored the journalist, your hands clasped in prayer, "No, please. I don't want to talk about that film." You were there to speak about your role in Luigi Comencini's *The Imposter*, but this film clearly didn't pique her curiosity. You nicely insisted, without getting angry, and you spoke slowly, choosing your words carefully. "I'm always linked to it. Everywhere I go, I have *Tango* with me. Enough is enough." You tried to explain: "I did films before it. I would have done things regardless."

I'm not sure you believed this yourself—that you would have had a film career if not for *Tango*. But you repeated it often, as if you longed to make it an incontrovertible fact.

Tactfully, you attempted to find a way out of the conversation. "I prefer that we speak about *The Passenger*. This film is closer to me." The journalist didn't respond. You were no longer of interest to her.

Did you know that you were almost not cast in the film? You weren't Bertolucci's first choice. Legend has it that Bernardo Bertolucci originally wanted to do a story between two men before quickly abandoning the idea. At the time, he was a hot director. His film *The Conformist*, which starred Jean-Louis Trintignant and Dominique Sanda, was a great critical success. With *Tango* he wanted to show the dark side of the sexual revolution, exploring sex and violence between two people in a Parisian hotel: Paul, a run-down forty-seven-year-old man whose wife has just committed suicide, and a young woman named Jeanne.

In the beginning, Bertolucci hoped to re-form the couple from *The Conformist* and sought out Trintignant for the role of Paul. Trintignant declined, saying, "In your film they're having sex all the time. Sorry, but I just can't go nude." Sanda was pregnant at the time and turned it down as well. Next, Berto-lucci returned to Paris hoping to meet with the two biggest actors in France at the time, Jean-Paul Belmondo and Alain Delon. Never the type to waste time, Belmondo refused to even meet. "I don't do porn films," he said. Delon's response was more ambiguous but classic Delon—he said neither yes nor no. Bertolucci's casting process ground to a halt. And then a friend suggested Marlon Brando. The mythic actor of American cinema had lost his splendor. Older and heavier than he was in his prime, he had acted in a string of commercial flops, which placed him in the category of Hollywood "has-beens." He needed cash after having purchased a Polynesian island that had turned into a money pit. He didn't know it yet, but his resurrection was just on the horizon, percolating in the desire of two young filmmakers, Francis Ford Coppola, who thought of him for *The Godfather* in 1971, and Bertolucci, with whom he finally agreed to work.

Still, convincing Brando wasn't easy. The first meeting took place at the Hôtel Raphael in Paris. Bertolucci described the project to Brando as the story of a man and a woman who renounce their social identities and communicate only carnally, through their bodies. Brando knitted his eyebrows and grumbled but nevertheless agreed to watch *The Conformist*, returning to the United States with the reels in his suitcase. A couple of weeks later he called the Italian director and invited him to spend a couple of weeks at his home in Los Angeles to discuss it. After hours of discussion, Brando agreed to play Paul in exchange for $250,000 and 10 percent of the film's gross—

a colossal sum of money for the time. It was up to Bertolucci to find the lion's share of the funding.

The director first caught sight of you in a photograph with Dominique Sanda, who had become a friend of yours. His Parisian casting assistants tried to talk him out of casting you. "Everyone said that she's just a girl who spends all night dancing at Castel's," he recounted several years later. "No one saw in her what I saw, something wild behind the androgynous body with the enormous breasts." During your first meeting he asked you to get a breast reduction. You refused. It was your sole act of rebellion. From then on nothing would be asked, only demanded.

You hesitated to do the film at first, as you later admitted, since you "didn't totally understand the script," though you did recognize that it was audacious and daring. Your agent swept away your reservations. "You can't refuse a leading role opposite Marlon Brando!"

You're nineteen years old, about to embark on the most scandalous role of the 1970s. Your mother had to sign a waiver so you could accept the role.

The first time you meet Marlon Brando is on the Pont de Passy just as you're about to shoot a scene. You find it funny that he's wearing lifts in his shoes and think, *Oh, he's not as big as all that.* You're ready to do your job, afraid of nothing.

Your first scenes are with Jean-Pierre Léaud (the favored actor of Truffaut and Godard), who plays your fiancé. Bertolucci didn't want to put you face-to-face with the icon right away, fearing you would be intimidated. Unexpectedly, however, Brando is there. You perceive a childlike sweetness in him as he tries to put you at ease. The first question he asks is what zodiac sign you are. "Aries," you tell him. "Me too," he says. "Rising?" "Libra." "We'll get along just fine," he says, "which is good, because I believe we have a few intimate scenes...." He gives you a kiss on the cheek as a father would give to his daughter.

Your first real scene of the shoot takes place in a bed. Any doubt about the nature of the film is extinguished immediately. For the sex scenes, or any scenes with nudity, Brando requests a closed set and Bertolucci complies, making the set off-limits to anyone not directly involved with the film. Photographers and other onlookers wait on the sidewalk every day for the actors to appear. Some even rent apartments across the street, hoping to get a shot. Only the curious and stubborn Jeanne Moreau manages to break through the barricade. Throughout Paris, rumors spread that the Italian director is making something risky and disturbing.

Brando imposes rules and conditions for everyone involved with the film. He does away with the rigid hierarchy common to film production. It's out of the question for him that the crew should eat less well than the actors. During the breaks he offers drinks and sandwiches to everyone, paid for out of his own pocket. "He respected people," you say later. "No matter how big or small. I'll always remember him as a generous and genuine man."

Brando goes back to his hotel every day at 6:00 p.m. and refuses to work on the weekends. Bertolucci doesn't object. For you, however, there is no such reprieve. You film take after take until after midnight, and on Saturdays you film your scenes with Léaud. It's more brutal than a marathon. By the end of the fifteen-week shoot you're drained and exhausted and you've lost twenty-two pounds. The crew often find you in tears. Some try to comfort you with a word or a look, others say nothing, pretending not to notice. *She's lucky, this little unknown, sharing the screen with the great Brando. . . . She doesn't get to complain.* Only once do you dare protest to the director: It's too much filming, fourteen hours per day, every day. You later tell me that Bertolucci responded without even looking you in the eye. "You're nothing. I discovered you. Go fuck yourself."

The Italian director soon understands that he's sitting on dynamite. The crew members are made to sign confidentiality clauses. The pairing between you and Brando works well, and Bertolucci is jubilant. *The girl is docile*, he thinks, and the actor brings his wounds to the role with an intensity beyond the director's wildest dreams. Brando gives him advice about camera placement and actors' performances. Bertolucci is fascinated by the experience and authority of this Hollywood giant and happily submits to him. You observe their dynamic, intrigued, watching Brando take over. At the last moment you are brought in to shoot your scenes. Bertolucci no longer speaks to you, only to Brando.

The director is fixated on the cinematography. He wants the

film to be orange, the color of the seventies—of hippies, saris, and Indian spices. The color of the Californian sun, the symbol of energy and vitality. The first rushes are reassuring; they have the tint he's looking for, but he's not quite satisfied. In the apartment, with the shutters closed, he feels there's something missing, some climactic event that could transform the film from daring to a veritable object of scandal.

One morning, Bertolucci takes Brando aside and suggests a scene that isn't in the script. The men agree that nothing should be said to tip you off—that it's better if you are taken by surprise. Did you sense a particular atmosphere on the set that day, complicit looks between the director, actor, and crew? Or were you too tired by that point to question anything? Who thought of the butter? Was it Brando, as Bertolucci claims, or Bertolucci, as Brando insists?

Rolling, action . . . You and Brando are lying on the floor, dressed. Suddenly, Brando turns you over, roughly pulls down your jeans and, grasping a mound of butter in his hand, he shoves it between your legs while thrusting his pelvis against you. You fight, you scream and cry. It's impossible to escape; Brando's body is pinning you to the floor. Bertolucci keeps the camera trained on your anger and terror. There's only one take. Afterward Bertolucci says, "*C'est bon.*" That's good. It doesn't last long, but for you it's an eternity. Brando releases his grip and you scramble up, staring at the two of them with murderous rage. In your furor, you destroy the set: tear down the drapes, shatter a vase, a lamp; anything you can get your hands on, you smash onto the wooden floor. After, you go to your dressing room and remain prostrate for hours. The director couldn't care less; he got what he wanted. He couldn't have dreamed of better. "She raged against me, against Marlon, against all men," Bertolucci would comment years later, remembering the scene.

You come out of the filming shattered, sensing this one scene has marked you forever, like a bad tattoo you'll spend the rest of your life trying to cover up. It doesn't matter that the sodomy was simulated—it makes you feel dirty and violated. You don't understand that you could've prevented this scene from appearing in the film since it wasn't in the script that you had agreed to. You could've called a lawyer, filed suit against the producers, and made Bertolucci cut it, but you're young, alone, and poorly counseled. You know nothing yet about the rules and regulations of the film world. The perfect victim.

Rumors swirl preceding the film's release. It's the return of the great Brando! A beautiful, provocative newcomer lights up the film! Bertolucci has really gone too far! At the preview, a few weeks before Christmas, people rush to find a seat. During the opening sequence, a malaise settles over the audience. Jean-Luc Godard storms out after ten minutes, furious and outraged, yelling "Horrible!" You're waiting outside the theater and don't hear him. You're wearing jeans with boots and a coat that's too thin to keep you warm. You pace and stomp your feet to prevent them going numb, smoking cigarette after cigarette, listening to the muffled noises coming from the screening room. At the end, the audience departs the theater in embarrassed silence. They pass by without looking at you. There's only one person who approaches you: the actress Jean Seberg. She's fourteen years your senior, as fair as you are dark. You've seen her in Otto Preminger's *Saint Joan*, Godard's *Breathless*, and all of the Romain Gary films. You don't know it, of course, but the two of you have Marlon Brando in common. It was her admiration of Brando that had made her decide, at twelve years old, to become an actress.

Seberg, the American icon of French New Wave cinema, now only works in low-budget films. The fresh and luminous Patricia of *Breathless* has been ravaged by sad love affairs and a chronic, abysmal sorrow that she attempts to drown in alcohol. She divorced Romain Gary, and two years before the release of *Tango*, her baby daughter, Nina, died. In September 1979, after several previous suicide attempts, her naked body will be found wrapped in a blanket in the back of her white Renault on a street in the 16th arrondissement.

It's the first time you've met her, but she wraps her arms around you and holds you against her chest. She's small and bony like a malnourished child, but the warmth of her body feels familiar. She buries her face in your brown curls and whispers in your ear, "Take care of yourself."

The Last Tango in Paris comes out in theaters on the fifteenth of December 1972. It fails to pass the censors and receives the rating "forbidden for anyone under eighteen," which only piques the public's curiosity. Immediately it becomes the preordained object of scandal. Catholics mobilize, and a complaint is filed in Italy, which the far Left views as an affront to their freedom of expression. *Tango* becomes the latest symbol in an ancient fight between the guardians of a certain moral order and the defenders of the artist's right to create— the wet blankets versus the squeaky wheels. The Italian court condemns Bertolucci, Brando, and you to two months in prison with probation. Copies of the film are destroyed. For Bertolucci, the controversy is a triumph. His film has succeeded in garnering the passionate response he desired. It's discussed in bars and restaurants, debated by artists as well as elected officials. It's forbidden in the dictatorships of the Soviet Union and Franco's Spain. Democracies, on the other hand, make a point of defending it. The film is first shown in New York at only one theater, where tickets sell out a week in advance. You attend the American premiere, where you're applauded. It's your first taste of success, but you stay on your guard. It's hard for you to know what to think when you are as likely to be booed as you are to be showered with compliments. You're twenty years old and soon will become world famous.

Meanwhile, just as your career is taking off, Brigitte Bardot announces she will retire. She's had it with films. From now on she wants to devote her life to animals, insisting they are far better than humans. Although you're not completely surprised, you're worried. You don't bother to try to talk her out of it since you know there's no changing her mind. She goes on to say that she'll no longer live in Paris. She's moving to Saint-Tropez, where she vacationed with her family as a child and where she filmed her great success *And God Created Woman*. It will become her refuge. You leave her apartment on the Avenue Paul-Doumer unsure of where you will go next.

The release of *Tango* generates a mixture of discomfort and horror in your family. Your half brother, Manuel, six years younger than you, questions your father, Daniel Gélin: "Everyone's talking about this film, and they say that she's your daughter."

"It's not true," he lies. "She's just a young actress who's starting out."

In our home, we don't speak about the film. The first time I hear anyone mention it is on the playground when I'm five or six years old: a group of kids laugh and yell, "Pass me the butter!" At first, I pay no attention to them, though what they say confuses me. They repeat it, day after day, and I don't know why. Finally, I question my mother.

"It's because of the film," she snaps, annoyed, then quickly tells me not to worry about it.

This scene becomes your cross to bear. For your entire life you will have to endure unsavory jokes and cruel pranks. Once, in a restaurant, a waiter asks with an obnoxious wink if you'd like some butter. On an airplane, a flight attendant puts a pat of butter on your plate when you haven't asked for any. Without your permission, a dairy manufacturer puts your picture on their labels. In Rome, where you are filming René Clément's *Wanted: Babysitter*, you're insulted on the street. More than once you are physically attacked. Faced with this incredible psychological violence, you hide your pain behind a forced laugh and respond with a quip: "I only cook with olive oil."

The press can't decide what to make of you—whether to love you or to hate you. Feminists wage war over the film. According to them, it goes too far under the guise of sexual freedom. They believe that total submission to the desire of a man symbolizes the alienation of women. Pointing out your youth—the apple cheeks and the look of confusion in your eyes about what's being asked of you—they wonder if what was captured on film was not art but abuse. They underline the nearly thirty-year age difference between you and Brando and note that in almost every scene you're naked while he remains clothed. And then there's the infamous sodomy scene. Some sense genuine protest and suffering in your cries.

The women's magazines don't quite know how to cover the subject. They're mesmerized by your beauty, your wild mane of hair, and the open nudity. You worry and intoxicate them at the same time. *Elle* decides to have it both ways. The magazine publishes the feminist arguments against the film yet still asks to meet with you. The narrative of the beautiful cursed woman, who's sure to be punished for her audacity, proves irresistible.

I discover the *Elle* profile many years later, in the piles of faded magazines that my mother had saved at the country house. I'm not even sure how *Elle* ended up there, how my mother managed this indulgence at a time when my father imposed such austerity. In our home, reading *Elle* was considered a mindless, guilty pleasure. According to my father, the magazine concerned itself with inconsequential things—fashion, tropical vacations, beauty creams—while the organizations that Papa worked for, the poster in the living room about the glory of Viet-Minh, and the riot gear stored at the top of the cupboard (just in case)—these were supposed to change the world. The toys we played with were made out of wood or fabric that came from faraway countries whose struggles we supported. Plastic weapons were banned, as well as Barbie dolls, which were considered symbols of female objectification. Our bedtime reading had to do with what was happening in China. Politics dominated all conversation. And yet, somehow *Elle* magazine managed to intrude on this revolutionary order.

At the end of 1972, the *Elle* journalist Marie-Laure Bouly attempts to reconcile the public's fascination with Maria Schneider and the scandal of *Tango*, beginning her article with a systematic evisceration of the movie: "A tasteless film that further demonstrates just how far is too far." She goes on to describe the young actress, who seems oblivious, both a capricious child and a femme fatale dressed in an oversize fur coat bought at Kensington Market in London. She's free-spirited—too free. The journalist doesn't seem to have found much to sink her teeth into, so she sprinkles her feature with quotes taken out of context that she doesn't bother to explain. Then the story comes to an end with the sudden departure of the star. Bouly concludes: "Maria Schneider is already gone, probably for the best."

• • •

The release of *Tango* is an explosion whose shock waves consume you within a couple of weeks. Nothing has prepared you for what's coming. The insults on the street, the aggression and abuse, and then, conversely, the adulation and the fawning. Doors suddenly swing open, offers come from the directors everyone is dying to work with. There is suddenly too much of everything in your life, too much desire, too much temptation, too much violence and criticism. With the wild grasping of someone drowning, you fall back onto a clichéd pun to explain the excesses of your behavior. "*Il vaut mieux être belle et rebelle que moche et re-moche.*" "It's better to be beautiful and rebellious than ugly and ugly again." It's delivered with a sardonic smile, like you only half believe it.

Since the press has portrayed you as a wanton muse, you play the assigned role. You will be as beautiful and rebellious as is expected of you, electric and without boundaries. Your first public statements whet the appetites of the gossipmongers. A girl who has grown up too fast, who still has the bloom of youth, taking aim at everything. As a journalist now, I shudder when I read the interviews. You settle the score with your father, the untouchable icon of French cinema, with all the rage and sadness of a neglected child. This father who took so long to acknowledge you, who now, as his film roles dwindle, cozies up to the smoldering fire of your success. You take him down with an assassin's precision: "A bitter man jealous of his own son." Your famous costar fares no better. "The Brando myth? Whatever.

He's obsessed with getting old and pays special attention to his makeup. Every morning, someone has to go get him, otherwise he won't come. He's also slow and lazy. He never knows his lines, he just improvises. Between takes he goes back to his dressing room, supposedly to 'center himself.' Typical Marlon, a big drinker!" You say whatever you want as you go about, methodically dismantling your burgeoning career. The journalists laugh nervously, unsure how to respond.

You're in London when you receive a phone call from the famous Italian film director Michelangelo Antonioni. After the success of *Blow-Up* he's finishing *Zabriskie Point*, a film depicting the student demonstrations and sexual liberation in the United States, with an original score by Pink Floyd. Antonioni has seen *Tango* and wants you for his next film. Did you realize how lucky you were to have this honor bestowed upon you? Surely you must have.

At what point did you decide to sabotage everything? Antonioni comes to Paris to have a top-secret meeting with you. He chooses the luxury hotel the George V, no doubt to demonstrate how much he wants to work with you. You show up disheveled and probably stoned. "I didn't go to bed until five in the morning," you will explain in an interview, "and then I go and sit across from this old guy with tics. We make a little small talk. I respect him, but I wasn't all that impressed." You tell Antonioni that you have to go run errands. He offers to accompany you, probably seeing the walk as an opportunity to ingratiate himself with you. You decline and take off, leaving him alone on the sidewalk like a bothersome suitor. You just wanted to get the meeting over with. "All I could think about was going to sleep," you confess later.

Daniel Gélin wants to make his paternity official. He's just authored a collection of poetry. Poetry is a passion of his, aside from the theater and the cinema. He invites you to come with him to a signing of his book *Poems to Say*, and you accept—you always have a hard time saying no to him. The press are summoned for the occasion. You take your place beside him, at a plastic table with a pile of books in front of you. You're wearing a white denim jacket, your long bangs cover your forehead, and the rest of your hair falls loose all the way down your back. You look younger than ever with no makeup, the cherubic cheeks and full lips. If you're already taking drugs, it doesn't show in your face. In a photo taken on that day, your father is speaking to you, his eyes locked on yours, as you listen to him, timid and attentive, an expression of profound sadness in your eyes.

You are twenty-one years old, filming the new Antonioni film in London. The "old guy with tics" wasn't put off by your behavior. He came back and begged until you finally relented. Your costar is Jack Nicholson. After Marlon Brando, the red carpet of an international career has unfurled under your feet. The press calls the film "the most mysterious of the year." Even the title is a secret. The budget ($3.5 million) is considered huge for the time.

Catherine Laporte of *Elle* magazine comes from Paris to interview you. It's the first time you've done a proper "question and answer." You've been urged to avoid blurting things out during the interview and have promised not to say anything inflammatory. The meeting is at the Russell Hotel, where you are staying. When you arrive, it's ten in the morning and you are accompanied by your companion at the time, an American named Joan (Joey) Townsend, whom you have brought to keep you from blurting out anything you shouldn't. After twelve weeks of filming you're exhausted, and though it's early you're already doped up. If the reporter notices, she doesn't mention it, remarking only that you've lost a lot of weight since *Tango*. "It's fatigue," you say. You're spacy, but after everything you've been through during the previous year, you understand that you can't afford to slip up. You've made up your mind that from now on, cross your heart, you'll no longer speak ill of anyone in public. The journalist understands within the very first moments of the interview that you're not going to make this easy. A game of cat and mouse ensues in which you respond to her inquiries with the absolute minimum number of words:

—Do you like your work as an actress?

"It's not really work."

—What do you do when you aren't filming?

"I hang out."

—And when you are filming?

"I hang out then, too."

—Do you like to read?

"I never read."

—What would you like to do later?

"I don't know."

—Are you a serious actress?

"I'm not anything."

—Are you comfortable in your own skin?

"What do you think?"

—Do you like being interviewed?

"I have nothing to say."

Normally this is when the journalist gets discouraged. But Catherine Laporte persists. Maybe she thinks that eventually you'll relax and trust her. The magazine has sent her across the channel to get an exclusive story on an international star, and she won't give up so easily.

—Don't you think that the public would like to know you better?

"They can go to see my films. The rest isn't important."

—Do you go to films often?

"It depends."

‚—Are you a good audience member?

"I think I'm an ordinary spectator, but sometimes I notice the angle of the camera and wonder what the motivation of the actors is when they're acting in this or that scene."

—You see? You do take your work seriously.

"Maybe . . ."

—During filming, are you even-tempered?

"It depends."

—What do you want out of life?

"What a question! I don't want anything. I want to live in the moment."

—Is it hard?

"Sometimes I'd prefer to sell bananas in Naples."

—Do you have a hard time expressing yourself?

"It's a question of words. My vocabulary isn't good enough."

—Are you happy to be twenty-one years old?

"I don't care."

—Tell me about *Last Tango in Paris*.

"It's about people together who do stuff."

—And Brando?

"He's someone with a very strong presence. That's it."

—I read in a magazine that you bought a house in London.

"I haven't read that. I've been living in hotels for a year."

—Do you like that way of life?

"It's as good as any other."

—Wouldn't you like to have your own home?

"Yes and no. I have a hard time concentrating on things, but maybe later . . ."

It's a fiasco, the kind of story that usually gets killed, but the magazine publishes it as is. "She looks for the slightest reason not to speak" is how the journalist describes the failed interview. For the art, there's a photo of you taken on set during a break. There are twenty people sitting on a wide set of stairs that appear to lead into a church. You are on the first step. Sitting next to you is a person with long hair wearing trousers and sandals. They seem to be asleep, with their head down and their arms wrapped around their knees. You're in a beautiful dress that I assume is part of your character's costume, since I've rarely ever seen you wear anything other than jeans. Two slender legs peek out from under the hem. On your feet you wear ballerina slippers with ribbons circling up your ankles. Your face is sulky. You stare off in the distance with your head in your hand as if it's become too heavy for you to hold upright.

Maria is here, Maria is there. She's in London. She's in Morocco. She's in Los Angeles, she's in Rome. She's nowhere at all. She crosses oceans, travels across cities, stays in hotel rooms, one after the other with the money from the poisonous film burning holes in her pockets. She gives it away, to her friends, to dealers, to anyone who asks her for it. She spends it on plane tickets, clothing, on free drinks for random people in discothèques. She loses it and she loses herself. Maria follows lovers—a nineteen-year-old Pakistani boy whom she describes as "super-beautiful" and then discards after a couple of months for a reckless relationship with a druggie American photographer that she carelessly divulges to journalists. Her vow of discretion doesn't last very long, and anyway, isn't that what the world is waiting for, the details of Maria Schneider's sex life? "I'm incapable of fidelity," she concedes with a shrug. "People accuse me of being destructive, but it's not true. I love life. I love men and women." Maria is free.

She's not beholden to anyone or anything, except for the heroin, which she starts using right after *Last Tango in Paris* comes out, and which she now injects every day, more and more frantically, increasing the dose each time.

You have disappeared. My parents are worried. In the apartment I listen to their anxious voices as they phone people, trying to track you down. Friends and family are all called. "Where is Maria?" No one knows. And then, just like that, without warning, you reappear. One never knows what state you'll be in when you arrive. Sometimes you're happy and excited, regaling us with stories of your travels—all the latest parties and film projects—but soon you fall back into despair or pass out.

I don't understand why you're sleeping in the middle of the afternoon. You're on the wooden daybed with a black pallet that my father filled with kapok and cushions covered with Indian fabric. You sleep in funny positions, your dark curls obscuring your face, the metallic clinking from the London market bracelets suddenly falling silent as your arms go still. I look at my mother for some kind of reassurance. *She's not dead, is she? Is she going to die?* I don't say these words out loud. They're too serious, and I'm too young, but they are always there at the front of my mind. I'm terrified, but I keep it to myself. Still, Maman understands everything. She grew up with lies and malice and sadness. She knows how terror can inhabit the minds of little girls. "It's the drugs. She'll wake up, don't worry."

She takes me into the kitchen with the orange plastic furniture and purple armchairs. There's a glass of milk and a *pain au chocolat* heated up in the oven just like every other day after school. She asks about my classes and then takes me to my room. I sit at my desk to do my homework. I'm not allowed to play until I've finished and everything is checked by her. After a bath we have dinner, then a story before bed—always at the same time—and then sleep. In this family where madness and unhappiness are never far away, Maman has installed strict rules and rituals. It's as though she believes that deviating from them for even one moment will plunge us all into chaos.

You are not yet thirty years old when you overdose and are committed to the Sainte-Anne sanitarium, where addicts are sent when going through withdrawal or suffering dementia. Patients are put in straitjackets and knocked out with high doses of medication. Some are given electroshock therapy. The families all know the drill. They navigate the maze of white corridors by rote under the fluorescent lights, trying to ignore the anguished cries escaping the rooms. They know the names of all the nurses; they know the medications and their doses.

By this time, you're shooting four grams of heroin a day, and have become a regular here. Your fame lends you VIP status. You receive a blood transfusion, a treatment that apparently is only ever administered to American celebrities near death. I'm eight years old and when I hear this I think it's super cool that you're being treated like such a huge star.

On this particular day, you seem calm. The pills have taken their effect. You asked Maman to bring you your pastels because you say you want to make art again. For a long time, you told stories in color—in pastels, felt-tip markers, and watercolors. When you were little, you drew women and men wearing intricate colorful fabrics, your lines precise in the manner of Japanese prints. I learned later that it was your stepfather, a painter, who taught you how to draw. As you got older, my parents collected your work and encouraged you to make more. You drew couples, princesses and princes, brides, dancers. You drew on greeting cards and restaurant menus and sold them between gigs as a film extra. Sometimes you drew scenes from film shoots, images from your life on set, actors in the middle of a scene. You used Chinese calligraphy ink, which made your sketches fine-lined and delicate. You could spend hours on the fabric of a dress or a man's doublet.

After *Tango* you stopped drawing. We preserve the last vestiges of your extinguished passion at the farmhouse. As a girl, during gloomy weekends in the country, I spend my time contemplating your work, which is stored in a cardboard box away from the light. One detail that particularly intrigues me is how you've given all the people very long necks, like giraffes. It's a strange and audacious proportion, calling to mind Modigliani's women or Giacometti's sculptures. Maman explains to me that's what it means to be a great artist, to be able to bypass formal rules and good taste, but I suspect that there was something more to it. Your creatures wanted to see farther than the others, to somehow peer at the secrets that lay beyond the horizon.

Today, in the hospital, my mother arrives with her arms full of art supplies. You manage a tired smile. You had made the same request of your own mother, but she had dropped off only a few used colored pencils. "Look," you say to my mother, gesturing sadly at the scatter of pencils on your night table. Soon your sadness shifts into rising anger. You repeat that you can't stand the closed room, the bars on the windows, the locked doors. You feel trapped. As Maman leaves, you begin to shout in rage, "I want to kill!"

It's a cold and rainy day in autumn. You're lost and looking for a helping hand. On this day, you find it in Frédéric Mitterrand, whom you know only a little. Though you come from different worlds, the two of you are kindred spirits. Mitterrand is an engineer's son, and the nephew of the future president of the Republic. A former student of the Sciences Po (The Paris Institute of Political Studies), he dropped out to pursue his passions, which are the same as yours: cinema, parties, excess. After he left school in 1971 he bought a movie house, L'Olympic, in the 14th arrondissement which was to be the first link in a chain of arthouse cinemas. Classic and independent films, all the cinematic masterpieces that can't be found anywhere else, are screened at L'Olympic. The movie house attracts cinephiles as well as a host of people from the fringes of society, including addicts of all kinds. It becomes a place to deal and get high, as well as a purveyor of odd jobs for otherwise unemployable young people, most of whom take the few francs they earn as ushers during the day to blow it on drugs at night. You and Mitterrand had crossed each other at L'Olympic previously but had never spoken. But he knows who you are, and you know who he is, and that's enough.

The day you go to the L'Olympic to find him is the first time the two of you actually speak. You're alone and agitated, and you ask him to lend you a few francs for a taxi. He wants to help but you tell him you don't need anything else. It's obvious you're in trouble.

"When someone travels across Paris to ask a stranger for such a small favor, it's a cry for help," Mitterrand will write many years later. He confesses that he gave you the money without asking for your phone number, not wanting to get ensnared in the complications of your life. "I was relieved to see her go. Her distress scared me." He watches as you stumble away in the pouring rain, deep in the throes of withdrawal.

There are few people who admit to fearing the madness of others and fleeing in the face of it. Mitterrand put into words our family's ambivalence—the rush of relief, and the attendant shame we feel when we don't hear from you.

Whenever you come to visit, my five-year-old brother hides in his room and refuses to see you. My parents don't insist. His meals are brought to him where he waits in the tipi set up next to his bed. He leaves the tent to go to the bathroom only after verifying that you aren't in the hallway. Sometimes you notice his absence. "The little one isn't here?" you ask. You barely listen to the response, having already moved on to something else, a story to tell, an urgent telephone call to make, a friend to meet, and then suddenly you're off. One day you ask, "Is he afraid of me?" as if you've only just then made the connection between your presence and his absence. You suspect the answer, and it bothers you. "He's just a child," my mother explains, as an excuse. You turn to me. "And you, you're not afraid of me, eh? I don't scare you, do I?" I shake my head and cling to you like a vine with my skinny arms, slipping my head through your forest of hair to press my face against your neck. I shower the needle pricks on your arms with kisses so that you will believe me.

Of course, you do scare me, but I don't want you to know that. I'm scared when you lose control and scream furiously, scratching yourself all over, tearing at your skin until you bleed. I'm scared because you fall asleep out of the blue, as though all life has left you, and then you scream yourself awake again, get up abruptly, and stagger around. I'm scared because you fight with people on the phone, switching back and forth between rage and maniacal laughter. I'm scared because of the things you say or do, and the way you move. The people you talk to, the ones we pass leaving school, or loitering in the stairway, the ones we see running errands at the supermarket or riding in the Métro— none of it is normal. It scares me, but I don't hide in my room because my desire to see you is stronger than my fear. When you're around, I don't want to miss anything. There's no one like you. Everything in your life seems extraordinary, your supply of stories inexhaustible. You spend nights dancing with Nathalie Delon and other people whose names mean little to me at my age but who I know are famous. You're photographed around Montparnasse at Castel's, wearing a boyish leather jacket and worn-out jeans. You get in fights and the next day remember nothing, though you're striped with blue and brown bruises. You tell us that your place in Rome was bombed by angry dealers. That one really makes an impression on me: an explosion, just like you would read about in the papers! There's nothing left, absolutely nothing, you say, before bursting into laughter. You're often robbed, and all your money stolen. After you leave our apartment, I question my mother, asking if everything you said is true. Maman purses her lips, not sure how to respond. She sometimes seems to doubt the things you say, but it doesn't matter. Even in our home, so far away from where the rest of your life unravels, you are constructing your own mythology.

On the morning of your death, the newspaper *Libération* prints a big, bare-chested photo of you obviously pulled from *Tango*. With your naked breasts on display, you appear as a carnal, sexual object. You had spent most of your life trying to erase this indelible mark, and you would have hated this kind of homage. It would have enraged you and made you cry. We didn't like this representation of you either, seeing you reduced to your flesh, because there is so much more to you than your exposed body, because the deceased should not be represented in such a way, because a newspaper would never dare to accompany the obituary of a man with a naked image of him, and last because *Libération* was not just any paper. It was the one my parents had bought every day since its first edition in 1973, the paper that initiated all of us children into politics. It was the paper that inspired me to become a journalist, the one where I worked for thirteen years and where one of my cousins still writes. It was not from this source that we anticipated a blow.

My brother and I are leaving school, our backpacks strapped onto our shoulders, when you appear, looming large in the middle of the crowd of parents—disheveled hair, a shearling coat thrown over a vintage blouse, the ever-present bangles jangling on your wrists. Your arms are raised high into the air. Maman stands beside you, holding a bag with a *pain au chocolat* from the boulangerie, as she does every day. In a matter of seconds the air is buzzing with the news: *That actress, the one in the scandalous film with Brando, is here!* Kids, parents, and teachers come out onto the porch to see what's going on. People jostle on the sidewalk to get a better view. In this quiet middle-class neighborhood it's not every day you see a celebrity, outside the pages of a magazine at the hairdresser's.

You don't look well. Your gestures are messy, your voice far too loud, your speech slurred. The most prudent mothers whisk their children away quickly, as though it's dangerous to stay. I see the children's faces as their heads crane around to gawk at us as they go, their eyes wide and glassy, struggling between having seen too much and wanting to know more. Maman tells you calmly that we have to go home now. You look at her in confusion. You don't seem to remember what you're doing there. When we get back to the apartment, my brother immediately locks himself in his room. In the kitchen, you spin round and round like a coin flicked across a table. You're speaking, but I don't understand what you're saying. I don't know if you're happy or angry. Maman offers you a glass of water, a cup of tea, whatever you want, whatever you need. At first you say "yes," then "no," then "I don't know." You're not listening. It appears you will sit, but then you jump up to pursue some irrational mission. You leave in a rush, without saying goodbye, calling out something along the lines of "Be right back." Soon we hear the screaming again. This time it comes from the concrete esplanade that joins our building to the others in the complex—the place where the kids play and the adults read their papers in the spring. From the window I can see you dancing and yelling. I'm not sure if you're singing or crying. The windows of the buildings open one after the other as families strain their necks to get a better look. Maman whispers in my ear, "She doesn't realize what she's doing."

All I can think about is the next day, the looks and mockery I'll have to endure from my schoolmates. It's not enough that my mother is mixed race, that we dress like clowns, now everyone knows, beyond any shadow of a doubt: My family is crazy.

And yet the shame is intertwined with pride—the pride of not being like everyone else. When I'm with you, I feel superior to the rest of the world. I belong to a tribe of people with extraordinary personalities, rich with an uncommon history. Sometimes I feel people pity us, but over the years, I begin to notice that we are also envied. Our family's drama makes us stand out from the humdrum crowd. Other people's lives pale in comparison. You feed our family's singularity. You tell us you once made love with Bob Dylan on an airplane, and the flight attendants had to separate you. The other passengers were so shocked that they threatened to file a complaint against the two of you upon landing. You still laugh about it as you imitate their expressions. "What puritans these Americans are!" Bob Dylan has a crush on you and you act like it's not important, but at the same time, you obviously want us to know. You tell us he wrote you a song. You make us listen to it and say that your photo is on the album cover. On the back of the album, there's a collage of snapshots: blurry faces, images of parties, the silhouettes of men and women with their bowed heads focused on something out of frame. I strain my eyes searching for your face in the images, and am finally convinced that I see you under a mass of brown curls.

• • •

In between these apparitions, life's equilibrium returns. Maman speaks very little, but cries often. I tell myself that it's because of her parents, who she tells us were mean. She stopped working after our births and organizes her schedule around ours, adhering to it with a strict discipline. She has psychoanalysis sessions where I imagine she spends the time talking about her mean parents. Papa works all the time. He's not satisfied with being a high-ranking official or with having earned the most prestigious diplomas; eventually he will become a psychoanalyst, a writer, and a literary and music critic as well.

In high school I'm considered a good student, and the teachers like me. In college I'm less studious, but the boys like me. Outside of my intimate circle of friends and lovers, I'm paralyzed by a crippling shyness. I hide behind a curtain of long brown hair and never raise my hand in class. The prospect of being called to the board plunges me into a pit of anxiety. When occasionally it does happen, my legs wobble underneath me, and I break out in a cold sweat. I open my mouth to speak and nothing comes out. In school I want more than anything to be forgotten. I try everything to make myself invisible and never do anything to make myself stand out. Never.

When I turned three years old, the age when school starts, I stopped eating meat. The mere sight of it cooking in a pan began to make me feel ill. My parents decide that it's not a big deal, but with the years, the list of things that repulse me grows longer. Fish, vegetables, salad, fruit. My "diet" poses problems for the staff of the Ministry of National Education, and my parents are often called in by the headmaster because I'm so skinny. (My mother prefers to call me "slim.") On the playground I fall down a lot, and I am regularly hit by bigger kids. Believing that I am the victim of bullying and malnutrition, Social Services summons my parents, who are more annoyed than worried. My father remembers not eating very much during his childhood before he learned to appreciate good food, and he believes that in the end the same will be true for me. At the time, though, I hear the term "infantile anorexia" without understanding its meaning. Today I wonder if I wasn't just trying to look like you.

I'm not a sad child. Life outside the housing project is full of joy. My best friend, Celia, has parents like mine. They live just next door, and we spend our time going back and forth between the two buildings. At my building, you have to buzz to gain entry. At Celia's, the key is left in the lock, even at night. Anyone—family, friends—can come in. In her home, you can draw on the walls and serve yourself ice cream from the big freezer in the hallway that leads to the bedrooms. In the living room there's a giant loom that her physician father works on from time to time, trying to make a carpet. In the kitchen, Celia's mother, Arlette, who insists on being called by her first name, serves lukewarm coffee to anyone who feels like chatting.

On Wednesday afternoons in winter, we girls ring the doorbell of the singer Renaud's brother. Renaud is our heartthrob. We swoon over his bleached blond hair, bowed legs, and black leather jacket. We feel he belongs to us more than to anyone else. The government housing that he sings about, where his brother lives, is where we live too. We know the characters in his songs—the redneck with the German shepherd and the neighbor on the fifth floor—and we were making fun of them long before Renaud's song about them became a hit. We're sure that if Renaud has chosen to write about us, we must be really special. He embodies the French youth of the moment, timid and arrogant, shattering the codes of disco and Variété (the mainstream music of France). He's like us, speaking in "verlan," the Parisian street kid slang. Those of us who are fluent use it to distinguish ourselves from those who haven't yet mastered it— it's *our* language. Our parents find the trend ridiculous. You can't mess around with the words used by the previous generation. To them, the words are still sacred.

Thierry Séchan answers the door and kindly greets us. He looks and dresses exactly like his brother. As a gift, he gives us red and white bandannas—Renaud's trademark look. Later, we will cut them into smaller triangles so we can share them with our friends. We leave our LPs with him and he promises to get them autographed for us. Thierry doesn't seem bothered by the stream of kids that come knocking on his door. When we're with him we have the impression we're with Renaud himself, and Thierry seems to enjoy sharing a bit of the spotlight.

Our parents allow us to wander the hallways, entrusting us to people they barely know. We sit on the couches in their one-bedroom apartments, where we're offered cookies and Oasis Tropical fruit drink. We go from block to block, sometimes with a jump rope, sometimes with metal roller skates, which make a terrible racket. We play "Chinese Jump Rope" between the buildings, attaching the rubber band to benches on the esplanade. Sometimes we go to the parfumerie to beg the saleswoman for samples of creams, which we slather on our cheeks. Eventually the owner of the store decides that we've come too many times and tells us to go elsewhere.

Celia and I share a passion for drawing and enter a contest organized by the school system. She wins first prize and I second. Arlette, a painter herself, has a very high opinion of our scribbles, and so one day we decide to sell them. We spend most of the afternoon fixing an astronomical price to each one. For discretion, we agree not to hit up our direct neighbors and instead go to another building in our complex, the one where someone (I don't remember if it was a man or a woman) threw themselves off the roof a few years earlier. As we climb the staircase we lose confidence, lowering our prices along the way. By the time we reach the doors, our swagger has completely evaporated. We end up drawing straws to decide who's going to ring the bell. In the end we sell all of our art and earn a couple of francs. We spend it buying candy that I'm strictly forbidden to eat, the kind that fizzles on the tongue, which Maman refers to as "poison." As soon as I get home, my breath betrays me. My mother insists it smells "chemical."

When the weather is good, we play on the esplanade. Our parents glance out the window from time to time to make sure everything's okay. We linger in the boutiques, pass by Madame Marouani's laundromat, and shop at the stationery store for school supplies. When we get tired, we set ourselves up in Celia's parents' Volkswagen van, which, like their apartment, is always unlocked. There's a mattress inside, where we lie and talk about our crushes, the careers we'll have when we grow up, all the places we'll go one day. We imagine the roads we'll take when we get our driver's licenses, all in the Volkswagen van, of course.

Some of the articles written about you during the height of your fame claim you are the daughter of Daniel Gélin and a "Romanian model." Your mother is Romanian only on her mother's side, but it doesn't matter. This is just one in a long list of errors that I will read about you.

No one in the family can recall that your mother was a model. However, everyone remembers that she was pregnant by the time she was fifteen years old and that the pregnancy was a stain on a family already plagued by scandal. During the pregnancy, she was locked away in "The Valley of the Wolves," a dilapidated sanatorium in Melun where she often roamed around in the nude.

Among the seven Schneider children, your mother's position was not ideal. The only girl in a family of boys, she was born a couple of years after the four "real Schneider children" and before the last two, who, like her, were born to different fathers. She grew up alongside her brothers in familial chaos, with a professional pianist and closeted father, who died too soon, and a violinist mother who died too late.

We didn't know your mother's father well, but everyone agreed that he was a lowlife who was suspected of having collaborated with the Germans during the war. In the grand bazaar of her existence, your grandmother tried in earnest to give each child a brother or sister from the same father. Your mother's only biological brother was a fragile man who was often taken advantage of. An alcoholic and petty thief, he returned home broken after the war in Algeria, put a rifle to his head, and killed himself.

I once rendered this familial tableau in a book you didn't like. You felt our family's history was personal—the alcoholism and madness, suicides and psychiatric hospital stays, ostracization and sexual orientation were nobody else's business. You'd probably hate that I am writing about it again.

You and I are on a train bound for Strasbourg. It's years after all the drugs and the screaming and fighting. Those left of my father's family—my uncle and aunt and a handful of cousins—sit together in an old second-class compartment, long before the high-speed trains accelerated travel through Europe. We are going to bury Henri, one of the last of my father's brothers and the only one without a biological brother or sister. He was considered the black sheep of the family, the one his mother liked least. She never mentioned him by name, and he's in none of the family photos. Henri didn't come to Paris. He lived his life in the Alsatian countryside in eastern France, surrounded by horses. Perhaps I met him once, probably at someone else's funeral. If so, I have no recollection of it. I didn't know much about him other than that he was a factory manager with no romantic relationships.

You sit facing me in the train compartment. Your mane of heavy curls cascades down your emaciated shoulders, and you hide the emerging wrinkles on your forehead with unruly curtain bangs. We talk about everything and nothing. You joke, employing your gallows humor as you often do to mask your anxiety. We don't know who from outside our family circle is going to be there, and we're both a little worried. I tried to avoid the trip, sensing it would be tedious, but my father insisted that

I go. "That's what it means to be a family, to show up together at funerals, even if the bonds have been broken," he told me. His urging was enough to convince me. At the train station we're picked up by people who introduce themselves so quickly that we don't catch their names. The day is a blur. There's mass in the church, then the burial at the cemetery, and then a drink at the home of the departed. A lot of people have come to say goodbye to Henri. He wasn't nearly as alone as I had imagined. It reassures me to think that the cursed brother had been loved by friends and colleagues, all these people who speak to us in an accent we find difficult to understand.

Henri's estate is substantial. My father had come the previous week to divvy up the inheritance. We draw straws like it's a game at a children's party. I get a collection of engraved sterling silver fish. Someone tells me it's worth a lot of money, but for fifteen years the fish will sit in a bag at the bottom of a closet. I still don't know what to do with them.

Your younger brother Eric arrives late, showing up when it's time for the toast. I've never met him before, and he makes me feel ill at ease. He's nice, but nervous and feverish. He's clingy, and already the small talk is exhausting. The cousins gather around the buffet and drink a few glasses of Alsatian wine in the hopes of relaxing a bit, but Eric monopolizes the conversation, repeating over and over how happy he is to see us. He says that we, "the kids," should go on holiday together. That it's so "cool" to finally meet. We can't lose any more time, he insists, we must absolutely get to know each other better. He suggests we rent a sailboat, assuring us that he knows how to sail, that the sea is his passion. Everyone nods, a little embarrassed. He seems so fragile, and no one wants to put a damper on his enthusiasm. One of my cousins surreptitiously whispers in my ear, "Can you imagine being stuck on a sailboat in the middle of the ocean with him?" We laugh foolishly. A little while later I hear about Eric's death. He went out for a walk and threw himself off a cliff into the ocean that he loved so much.

At the end of the afternoon, after our uncle is laid to rest, our main concern is that we not miss the train back to Paris. No one says it aloud, but it's understood that spending even one night there is inconceivable. You seem especially intent on not getting stranded. We search for someone willing to take us to the station and several guests volunteer. I sit in the back of a car with you. Earlier, the couple driving us had bombarded us with questions, curious about exactly how you were related to them. The husband brought up some names that we were supposed to know, searching for the enigmatic familial tie. We responded to their interrogations as politely as we could, but the vagueness of our replies disturbed him then—and does so again now. The ride is tense. Through the window I try to spot signs that might indicate how much longer the trip will be. Our drivers still don't seem ready to let us off the hook. After a while, the woman turns to face us, an accusing look in her eye. "So, actually, you don't know *any* Schneiders?"

When we are kids, our parents make sure that my brother and I experience all the quirks that are in vogue in the seventies. The way we live is completely incongruous considering my father's professional status, as well as my parents' upper-middle-class origins. We live in low-income housing paid for by the state because my father is the sole breadwinner for a family with two children. We spend our weekends in a shared house near the Rambouillet Forest. For summer vacations we camp for weeks on a wild and windy Breton island in the North of France, where we sleep on inflatable mattresses and don't even think of bathing. Sometimes we join friends in stone ruins high in the Cévennes mountains. The ancient houses are at the end of a long and treacherous path. They're stifling with no running water or electricity. From time to time my mother's cousin and her chiropractor husband join us. He brings a pendulum that he uses to locate bad energy and evil spirits. They're vegans who have renounced all nourishment from animals: meat, fish, milk, and eggs. I still remember the bitterness of the Swiss chard tarts and bulgur salads served at every meal. The adult conversation revolves around subjects such as the effect of the full moon on hair growth. My father isn't particularly interested in the paranormal or the other big questions of the universe that concern the hippies we socialize with.

My mother buys the majority of her clothing at flea markets.

She adorns her outfits with jewelry that she makes herself. Brass pins covered in glitter, iridescent beads that shimmer against her dark skin, dangling earrings that tangle in her frizzy hair. She occasionally sells these painstakingly crafted objects to boutiques, or gives them to those closest to her, to her sister-in-law and to you, Maria. You love them.

She dresses my brother and me in a mixture of clothes purchased at the discount store called Prisunic and items brought back by friends from all the corners of the world: embroidered peasant blouses, Indian saris, Peruvian bonnets, Danish clogs, itchy hand-knitted sweaters in brightly colored wool mixed with satin ribbons and Lurex threads. In photos from this era, we are a sight to behold. Dark sparkling eyes, long bushy hair, posing in our mismatched ensembles. At the time I hate the way we dress. The ill-fitting sweaters, the clogs that hurt our ankles and make games on the playground dangerous. We consistently lose at hide-and-seek and tag, because we're too slow to keep up. Skipping rope is nearly impossible.

It's with these small, seemingly insignificant things, at the age where all you want is to be exactly like everyone else, that the shame first trickles in. I dream of simple smocked dresses and strapped sandals, patent leather Mary Janes and pleated skirts, primary colors—blue, red, and yellow—instead of the garish purple, orange, and pink we usually wear. Finally, due to my stubbornness, my mother allows me to dress the way my friends do. By that time our means have also improved. Still, the shame lurks in the background, ready to emerge in violent, uncontrollable bursts. I've never gotten over the feeling of being different.

It was more than just our strange sartorial style; our clothing drew attention to a suspicion I preferred to ignore: something wasn't right with us.

The close-knit, if unconventional, quartet of my immediate family is not enough to protect us from the madness that surrounds us. While other children speak fondly of their extended families, their kind grandparents, aunts, uncles, and cousins, my paternal grandmother once passed out in the sanatorium from drinking the little bottles of perfume that her children had brought her as gifts. My paternal grandfather died when my father was a baby. My father's family lineage is so convoluted that we rarely dare to speak of it. When he turned twenty, my father discovered by accident that his father wasn't his biological father, nor, with the exception of one, were his brothers his biological siblings. Consequently, in our immediate family tree there are what are referred to as the "real" and the "false" Schneiders—a line of demarcation based on parentage and the erraticism of one's behavior. The "false" we never see. They are said to be "crazy"—alcoholics, drug addicts, lost souls. When we hear about them, it usually means there's been an argument, inevitably a very serious one, or a mental breakdown, or a brutal death. In the waiting room of an asylum, in the hospital, or in the cemetery we invoke this idea of the "real" and the "false," never knowing exactly which category we are in.

You, Maria, are somewhere between the "real" and the "false," in the indeterminate zone. If you are in the "crazy" category, you, at least, are thought to have excuses.

It's 2010 and you are very sick. When the tumor in your lung was diagnosed, more than a year ago, the doctors were very pessimistic about your chances. After multiple operations, you submit to several rounds of heavy radiation. You try new treatments that are thought to be more effective than the old ones. Up until the very end, you assure us in a progressively weakening voice that you will get better. You lose weight, cut off your beautiful hair, and stop coloring it. The treatment exhausts you, and you're plagued by an unrelenting cough. Yet still you insist you'll recover. You cite the cases of acquaintances who survived after being told they were doomed. Your certainty persists, even after you leave the apartment in the Palais-Royal for a hospice from which patients only ever leave in a shroud.

We all go to see you, individually, so as not to tire you out. You no longer eat very much. When asked what would make you happy, you invariably reply "Champagne." You love the finest ones with the fancy labels and the small bubbles—the sound of the flutes clinking against each other. We always share a glass or two, no matter the hour of day—you pretending to hide it, as though you're a naughty child, which makes the nurses smile. You like your room because it's clean and spacious. The gifts people bring you are placed on the windowsill. Some remain wrapped; either you're too tired to open them or you can't see the point, probably because deep down you know you'll never bring them home. In time it becomes more and more difficult for you to get up, but you always ask to accompany us to the door.

The night before you die, you point up at the recessed spotlights in the ceiling and smile, your face briefly illuminated. "Just like a film set."

Brigitte Bardot insists on covering the cost of your funeral. The family has no say in the matter. For as long as I can remember, you spoke of "Brigitte," and it was always understood that you meant Bardot. When you become ill, you get back in touch with her despite the decades of silence between you. Had you felt abandoned by her when you had to leave her apartment on the Avenue Paul-Doumer, after having so recently left my parents' home? I never hear you speak about it, since you prefer not to dwell on the sad moments in your life. You tell us instead about the reestablished bond between you, the regular Sunday telephone calls and all the gifts she sends you. Your fame was not comparable to hers, but you had suffered in similar ways—actresses branded as "sex symbols," whose artistic talent, it seemed, was never the point of interest. Both of you had careers shaped by male dominance.

In the end, Brigitte asks what would make you the most happy, and you respond without hesitation: "To return to Menthon-Saint-Bernard." You're remembering a vacation home our family once owned but I never had a chance to see. Our age difference has provided us with distinctly different family geographies. The family residences in Melun and Menthon were swallowed up by bankruptcy before I was born. You cherish the memories of the house on the shore of Lake Annecy where you spent most of your childhood summers. Brigitte gifts you the trip to the Alps, both the train and the hotel. "She only cares about broken stray dogs," you joke.

Maria Schneider is a guest on *Cinéma Cinémas*, a talk show by the film critic Michel Boujut and the director Claude Ventura dedicated to actors and directors. The program lasts seven minutes and forty seconds. It's unlike any other television show, a series of interviews put together like little films, where the camera remains trained on the subject. Subjects can drink, smoke, bend down, turn their heads, or move out of frame altogether. The filming continues during the silences. The construct is of a subject turned actor in a film about themselves—of reality turned to fiction.

You're seated on a banquette in a café, your mass of hair reflected in the enormous mirror behind you. The baby fat has been replaced by the more mature and angular beauty of a woman in her thirties. Silver hoop earrings flicker against the auburn highlights of your hair. You wear your uniform—a black jacket over a white collarless blouse. I assume you're wearing jeans, but your legs are hidden under the table. You're sitting up straight.

First cigarette: The sequence begins in the middle of a discussion as though the viewer has just happened onto a conversation between two people. You use the familiar *tu* with the interviewer, who remains offscreen. You're discussing the inequality of men's and women's treatment in the film world. You never use the word "misogyny" and don't identify yourself as a feminist, saying only, "It's easier for men. They're considered entertainers. When you see the fate of people like Romy [Schneider, no relation] or the others, it makes you wonder." Pause.

Second cigarette: "I turn down a lot of roles. There aren't a lot of dignified female roles. It's always the women who exist only in relation to the man, or to the couple." After a moment you continue: "Like everywhere else, in film it's the men who have the power." You say it simply, resigned, fatalistic. You take another drag and exhale. The smoke blurs the image and you fall silent. You don't speak lightly. This question of status, yours and that of all women, bothers you.

Just seven years earlier, when you were twenty-three years old and the critics were still predicting your brilliant future, you expressed a deep pessimism in a documentary entitled *Be Pretty and Shut Up* directed by the actress Delphine Seyrig. Twenty-four actresses and female directors, French, English, and American, are interviewed regarding the place of women in film. Your part is filmed in the country, surrounded by overgrown foliage that looks as though it's going to swallow you up. You smoke furiously as you talk. "I only get the roles of schizophrenics, crazy women, or angry lesbians, which I don't really feel like playing right now." You say you'd like to be offered something lighthearted, a project with a little joy. "I'd love to do something more fun. A film like *Céline and Julie Go Boating* [a quirky 1974 comedy about female friendship by Jacques Rivette]." You laugh and continue. "Also, something with a man who's around my own age! Nicholson was better than Brando, but not much. He was forty years old. I was twenty-three. The producers are men. The crew are men. The directors, for the most part, are men. The press is men. The agents who give you the scripts and advise you are men, and the scripts themselves are all just vehicles for men."

In front of *Cinéma Cinémas'* camera, ten years after *Tango*, you seem to understand several more things. "It's a very dangerous job." You're emphatic on this point. "Very. It's a job I wouldn't advise any young person to do. You have to be strong mentally in the head." In the background the hissing of a coffeemaker mixes with the sound of someone aggressively slamming the flippers of a pinball machine.

Third cigarette: "When you were little, did you want to be in films?" You shake your head no. "I wanted to draw, to become a painter." You're distracted by another loud noise in the room. "What, is there an organ grinder in here?"

There are two opposing theories in our family about why your career was so brief. The first one, and the one that circulates most in our home, is that it was the drugs. The second, and the one to which you cling most stubbornly, has to do with the violence of the film world, where all the rules are dictated by men. But there's a third reason, less often discussed but communally felt: that it just wasn't for you. You loved movies—perhaps in part because they were an invisible thread that connected you to your father. But acting, actually playing parts—you could take it or leave it.

• • •

Toward the end of the seven-minute-and-forty-second sequence dedicated to you, the interviewer asks one last question:

"Do you like being on set?"

You smile almost as if you are masking embarrassment. You lower your eyes. It lasts only a fraction of a moment, but in your brief silence I perceive a confession. Then, you raise your head and look insolently into the camera—your typical bravado on display.

"If I didn't like it, I would've done something else."

You're sprawled out on the couch. You seem to be asleep but then quickly get up, agitated, and scratch yourself as though you've just been attacked by a swarm of insects. You scratch your skin so furiously I'm afraid that you're going to hurt herself. You grab your bag and say you must go immediately. You're going into withdrawal again and want to go find a dealer. Even though my parents have tried to explain this scenario to me numerous times, they try again. The door slams without a goodbye, as usual. A few minutes later you're back, angrily ringing the bell and banging on the door with your fists because we haven't let you in fast enough. You're furious because your moped, the one you bought only yesterday, is gone. You had come over just to show it off, and we had all made the trek downstairs to admire it. You were so proud that I teared up along with you. I fawned over the blue metallic paint and the chrome on the rearview mirror. It may have been the most beautiful moped in the world.

You're outraged that someone could've stolen it, but my father points out that it wasn't locked up and that you may even have left the keys in the ignition. You protest but are unable to find the key fob. You continue railing against "this shit neighborhood," grumbling that you don't even know why you bother to come here. Key or no key, you insist, it isn't normal for someone to have just stolen it. You want to go to the cops and press charges.

"They'll see what they get, those little bastards!"

My father tries to talk you out of it, but he's starting to lose his patience—with your antics, with the endless crises, with the drugs. He'd like to spend one weekend in peace for a change. Once more he attempts to calm you down.

"Maria, you can't go to the police station in your state."

You don't understand and protest. "I don't see why not!"

Exasperation and fear outstrip Papa's patience. He too starts to yell and grabs you by the arms, brutally rolling up your sleeves while you struggle.

"You still don't understand? Look at yourself! Look at your arms! You think the cops are just going to take your report and then let you go like that?"

He points to all the track marks. I'm a child, but I'm right there and I look. There are so many—I didn't think there could be so many—as well as bruises and skin lesions. He drags you over to a mirror and lifts your heavy mane of hair, pointing to the red dots and yellow lines on your neck.

"You're covered in holes, from head to toe! Look at yourself," he repeats over and over. "Look! Look!"

You keep your eyes shut, and I close mine too because it's too ugly to watch. My head is spinning. Finally, you're quiet.

Papa seems exhausted as he lets you go. "Go ahead if you want." His voice is so low, it's barely audible. "But I won't be coming to bail you out."

You take off. In the stairwell we hear one last cry. "You'll never see me again!"

A few days later, you're back, sprawled against the Indian

cushions with a scarf wrapped around your neck and a glazed look in your eyes. The blue moped is forgotten.

We're driving in our white Renault R12, the car we kept until it died. I'm looking out the window, which is slightly open, the way Maman taught me to avoid carsickness. I always feel like I'm going to throw up in this car. The sticky leatherette seats reeking of cigarettes combined with a suspicious odor emanating from the trunk never fails to nauseate me. Papa can't throw anything away, saying it's because he's a child of the war. We roll our eyes when he says this since he was born in the spring of 1944, and the only war he's known is in the stories told by his elders. But still, he can't get rid of anything. Leftover chicken or a couple spoonfuls of soup, a piece of moldy cheese and a few slices of bread—he always insists on schlepping the scraps back with us to Paris in plastic bags, which inevitably break and spill in the trunk. The foul odor grips me every time I take my place in the passenger seat. It's compounded by the fact that, other than summer vacation, we typically only use the car to go places I hate: the house in the country, or Saint-Maur to visit my grandmother, who waits in a nursing home for death to release her from her miserable life.

Today we're going somewhere new. I see the city slipping away, the suburbs stretching out as detached houses replace the apartment buildings. The countryside emerges—a tapestry in shades of greens and gold, dotted with little villages that disappear as quickly as they appear.

As we drive to this unknown destination, I'm not thinking so much of the putrid smell of the Renault. Instead, I think about drugs—the drugs that have become the center of everything. Every time you return to our home you're more strung out, more damaged than last time, and every time you promise to stop, but don't. We watch you killing yourself before our eyes. The days spent at Sainte-Anne were only a brief lull in the nightmare of your addiction. You escaped as soon as you could to run and find another fix. Papa heard about a clinic tailored to the needs of heroin addicts and tried to convince you to go, but you didn't want to since it's so far from Paris.

So we are going to commit you, as a family, because we do everything as a family. When we arrive, my brother and I wait outside in the car while our parents walk you in. Your savage screams reach all the way to the parking lot where we sit waiting while inside the clinic you are forcibly restrained and then sedated. We return to Paris in silence with the echoes of your despair following us all the way home.

During the night, you escape from this institution and vow never to see Papa again.

I often worry that you won't approve of the story I'm telling, Maria. You won't like that I'm speaking of the drugs, of your mother and father and brothers. So, I erase what I just wrote, and then I write it again, because talking about you without talking about the drugs, your mother, your father, or *Tango* would mean giving up talking about you at all.

We should have done this book together. In fact, at one point we planned to. Once, during a Christmas dinner at my parents' house after your reconciliation with my father, you approach me about the possibility of writing a memoir with you. You aren't sick yet, but you are preoccupied with death, and with your legacy. You want to be the one to tell your side of the story, and confide that you have already filled dozens of notebooks with notes about your life on set and other memories, but that you can't do it all alone. Since I'm a writer, you ask if I would like to do it with you. Your partner A., the woman with whom you will spend the better part of your life, approves of the idea and encourages us, saying family can be trusted.

I promise to think it over. I sense that it won't be an easy project, and that concerns me. You still seem so raw and unpredictable. On the phone you reassure me, saying that you've thought about it long enough to not back out now. I reach out to my friend Judith, with whom I worked at *Libération*. She advises me to speak with Jean-Marc Roberts at Stock Edition: "The seventies, cinema, it's his thing," she tells me. I arrive at the publishing house on the Rue de Fleurus with the timidity of a novice, clumsily explaining myself, but he cuts me off. "No need to say another word, I love it."

I organize a meeting for the three of us at the Hôtel du Louvre, not far from your apartment. You love the ambience of hotel bars, the subdued lighting and attention to good service. The conversation between you takes off without my having to intervene. You exchange common memories of Paris nightlife and old, forgotten acquaintances.

Roberts gives us a fantastic contract and you seem excited, jubilant even. But very soon, the doubts creep in. *Do we have to talk about my father? Is it really necessary to mention the drugs? What will we say about my mother?* I try to reassure you, but the anguished phone calls multiply. The more you think about the book, the less you're able to sleep. The mere idea of conjuring memories plunges you into profound dread. Your doubts quickly transfer to me. The book shouldn't be a source of suffering for either one of us, so I decide not to do it. With relief you return the advance.

From time to time at family get-togethers, you allude to the book. You say you aren't ready yet, but one day you will be. I pretend to believe you, but in my heart I know that day will never come. I know that I'll have to write it alone. Not the story that you would write, which belongs only to you and of which I know so little, but ours.

I learned your filmography in a haphazard way. The first film I ever saw you in was *Memoirs of a French Whore*, in which you play a prostitute alongside the actress Miou-Miou. Her character is Marie, and you are Maloup. The director, Daniel Duval, plays Gèrard, the pimp. The 1979 film purports to examine the degradation and violence of prostitution, a world in which women are manipulated and humiliated by men, but to me it's just another film where you're naked and abused. Seven years after *Tango* you have still not managed to escape the prison of these roles. You're in most of the scenes, but your character says nothing, letting Miou-Miou's character speak for you. In fact, everyone in the film speaks except for you. I notice your silence but don't understand it. Later I'm told that most of your lines were cut because you were too high to manage more than a couple of sentences at a time.

The film is a hit at the box office, but for you, it's a turning point. You make it known that you no longer want to take your clothes off on film. By the beginning of the eighties, you are turning down any script that includes sex scenes. Still, the majority of offers you receive require nudity. You decline them all, often rudely. Sometimes you try to negotiate, agreeing to do the films if the scenes that embarrass you most are cut, but you lose every time. The roles are given to others and the scripts that once cluttered your mailbox stop coming. You're no longer considered for the starring roles, and then not for the supporting ones, either.

Because of the estrangement with Papa, you don't come to our home for several years, and I only see you at my aunt and uncle's place. At Chez George, as we call it, you're pampered, loved, and celebrated, no matter what you say or do. Our uncle is my father's sole biological brother and the closest to him in age.

The Georges are the only extended family members we see regularly. When I was a child, I felt that going to their home was a treat. For me, their apartment, beside the Montrouge cemetery, has a lightness and joie de vivre lacking in our home. Here, I can watch broad comedies or cheesy soaps on the television. My uncle has two grand passions, classical music and soccer, at a time when watching sports was not a common interest of the middle class. In summer, the Georges escape Paris for the South of France, Spain, or Italy, where they stay with my three cousins in places that my parents consider out of their price range. I'm always envious of the Georges' vacations. One summer they take me with them to a resort near Alicante where very early in the day, a giant building casts a cold shadow on the beach. When the sun disappears, we happily decamp for the pool at the residence. There's nothing that rattles the Georges, no obstacle that can dampen their good humor. I learn to have fun with them, to talk nonsense, eat Popsicles, do cannonballs in the pool, and lie in the sun too long. In the evenings after dinner, we take walks on the promenade and run to the street vendors to buy candy and trinkets. The weather is always mild. I discover for the first time that a place exists where you can be outside at night with your arms and legs bare.

The vacation is unforgettable. I adore my uncle and his way of finding joy in the simple pleasures of life, and my aunt, who spends her days preparing delicious meals for the family. After that trip, I'm certain that my cousins' lives are much happier than ours. I often spend the weekends in Paris at their place, sleeping on the sofa in the living room. We talk, watch films on the VCR, and listen to sports matches on the radio. My aunt prepares my favorite meal, lasagna with floating island for dessert. I'm not used to eating so much and every Sunday I return home a little queasy.

Later, the reason I want to spend time at Chez George is

that I get to see you. My aunt knows I am always eager to see my special cousin and invites me whenever she knows you'll be around. My mother often joins me. You're no longer shooting heroin; instead, you chain-smoke cigarettes.

As I enter adolescence, I discover a new you—calmer, without the outbursts or crises. Every year, the Georges have a party to watch the César film awards. The evenings are mellow, haloed in a marijuana mist. As the years pass, you still join us, but you're not the same. The heroin has left deep traces on your skin, like acne scars that never quite fade. Your hair has become dull and the drugs have ruined your teeth. Your curves are gone, and in their place the sharp angles of your body protrude under baggy jeans. Even your full mouth seems to have shrunk. Bitterness gleams on your face. You still have your sense of humor, but now you wield it to make fun of others—the actresses you're sure have had "work done," the ridiculous hype around others, actors who had once been your friends but haven't kept in touch now that you no longer have top billing. You don't say it and we pretend not to notice, but you must know that there's no future for you in film. You talk about the past, about the roles that were stolen from you—the ones you lost out on or claim could have been yours, had you wanted them. *One Deadly Summer* was one of the big hits you say you turned down. The lead role went to Isabelle Adjani instead, but you insist that you had been the first choice. The proof was that they curled Adjani's hair and styled it to look like yours. Luis Buñuel's *That Obscure Object of Desire* was another. He ended up hiring both Carole Bouquet and Angela Molina to play a role that was originally to be played by you alone, and this makes you proud. "He had to have *two* actresses to replace me!" you crow. You neglect to mention that you were fired after only four days of shooting because the drugs had made you impossible to work with.

When you aren't rewriting the past, you go on about the banalities of everyday life—your declining eyesight, financial problems, dental expenses, your too small apartment in the Palais-Royal. Sometimes there's a glimmer of your former splendor, a memory that lights up your eyes, a low husky laugh, a whiff of perfume that escapes from your hair.

Although the directors turn their backs on you, the press are more reluctant to do so. On June 9, 1978, *Paris Match* devotes four pages to you with the title "Lost Child of the Cinema." There's a picture of you sitting in a wild untended garden with your tousled mop of hair. You're wearing a shirtdress with a safety pin in place of a missing button. You squeeze your hands together, and your expression is pinched as though in response to a photographer who has just asked you to smile. Below the photograph is an unattributed caption: "One of the best actresses of her generation chooses a life far from it all in the middle of the woods, 500 kilometers from Stockholm." Not very glamorous. You're not the one the magazine has chosen to grace its cover. Instead, they chose twenty-five-year-old Isabelle Huppert, who is starring in Claude Chabrol's *Violette*. The actress, with an adolescent's freckles and hair the color of a sunset, lights up the page. She embodies an era determined to erase the excesses of the past. The young girl next door. Small, delicate, fresh-faced, and French. So very French. "Isabelle Huppert Triumphs at Cannes" reads the headline. Inside are pictures of Huppert, licking an ice-cream cone, or holding her hair away from her shoulders and swinging her hips. They are alluring poses, but she's fully clothed from head to toe. There's even a scarf tied around her neck. "Isabelle loves parks, public gardens and quirky provincial streets," the article informs us. This is a generation without scandal—no drugs or violent deaths. No drama.

By the end of the seventies there's a yearning for rest and a return to morality after years of wanton debauchery. *Paris Match* has taken it upon itself to set the record straight. This issue devotes the first five pages to "child smokers." "Our children begin smoking at age eleven!" the reporter announces with alarm. "Faced with smoking, teachers are cowardly and help-less." The article brings to mind a photograph my parents took of me. I must have been about four years old with bangs cut straight across my forehead. I'm in the garden at the country house wearing a bright green nightgown with TIME OUT—IT'S BEDTIME! emblazoned on it. Clearly, I'm not headed to bed. In my right hand I am holding a lit cigarette and in my left a hand-ful of candy.

The Soccer World Cup takes place in Argentina in 1978, while that country is still under the yoke of a fierce dictatorship. *Paris Match* sends the writer Jean Cau, who wishes to "penetrate the intimacy of the team." He notes that the players are divided. One member of the Argentine team, Dominique Rocheteau, seems uncomfortable and pensive. "We're complicit with the Argentine regime," he says while being massaged by the team's physical therapist. Another player, Michel Platini, doesn't seem to share Rocheteau's concerns. "It's no worse here than anywhere else," he says with a shrug.

In our home it's out of the question that we would watch a World Cup taking place in a country controlled by a military dictatorship. There's a large poster taped to our living room wall with the slogan "Boycott Argentina" over the image of a soccer ball enveloped in barbed wire.

It's been four years since Valéry Giscard d'Estaing was elected president of France, and *Paris Match* has never stopped celebrating. In this issue there's a series of flattering shots of him. Giscard being hosted by Jimmy Carter at the White House, greeting Jackie Onassis on the Concorde, making conversation with Paul Newman. Giscard, the modern president, who changed the voting age from twenty-one to eighteen, and who gave women the right to their own bodies. In 1978, on the anniversary of his election, Giscard celebrates in a village in Haute-Savoie where he got 92 percent of the votes. "Giscard blows out the four candles in front of the priest, the headmaster, and others," reads the caption. A few pages in, under the social gossip, we learn that his son Henri "very much likes the punk club La Palace, the livelier the better." How incredible the Giscard d'Estaing family is! Protectors of the old France, the teachers and the church, but also so au courant! The coverage is pure propaganda.

The four pages in the magazine dedicated to you are in black-and-white, as if to evoke your tragic destiny. This era has chosen its new stars, and they're solid, and subdued. They aren't drifters. The piece on you is there to remind readers that everything must be paid for eventually, that sexual freedom will only lead to destruction and despair. Ten years later it's determined that the demonstrations of May 1968 caused more harm than good. *Paris Match* readers can look at photos of the lost actress from the comfort of their modern homes and say to themselves, "Thank God that's all behind us!" You are described as a sort of Brigitte Bardot of the flower generation. No clichés are spared: "Lolita," "Provocative Bambi," "Cover Girl." Now that the drugs have taken away your career, you're supposed to be in your "redemption phase." You say what's expected of you.

"Here, you just hear the birds, drink tea, eat fruit. . . . That's life. . . . But I don't know why I have to tell you this!" you say to the journalist, always wary of this question-and-answer game. "I don't need to justify myself. People can think what they want— that I'm a druggie, a dirty junkie, that I'm temperamental, I don't care." The article reports that you are in the company of a "top model," the ex-wife of jazz musician Quincy Jones. Your silhouette is graceful in a long skirt. You're standing up in the picture, next to a chaise longue in this wild garden with your arms crossed protectively in front of your body. Perhaps you're attempting to hide your increasingly frequent tremors, or maybe you're just cold.

Two more photos accompany the piece. There's a picture of you at age three, smiling, bundled up in a duffel coat that's a little too big for you. You're holding your mother's hand. She's wearing an Astrakhan coat and has bleached blond hair. Just underneath this picture is another of you behind bars, standing next to your friend Joey Townsend. "Maria, in a jail in Rome, joins another addict friend." At the end of the article the writer becomes lyrical, full of hammy emotion. "She was a child pushed too soon into the spotlight. She didn't know the steep price she would pay for seducing the public. Now, who does she have to listen and heal her except for the trees?"

Other actresses aren't hiding away in the forest. In this same issue of *Paris Match*, they're shown at the Cannes Film Festival, in bathing suits on the beach, or in dazzling, glittery evening gowns. Seventeen-year-old Anne Parillaud poses in front of the Carlton, Geraldine Chaplin pouts attractively, Jane Fonda wears a Panama hat and a blouse open to her navel. Even Sylvia Kristel, star of the infamous Emmanuelle films, has remained in good graces. "She mellowed after getting together with the English actor Ian McShane," the magazine explains. "Kristel escapes to kiss her son, Arthur, who lives with his grandmother in Holland, while she's preparing to shoot a new film." A new relationship, a new film, and a child for Sylvia Kristel. Honor is restored, pronounces *Paris Match* breathlessly.

•   •   •

I'm twenty years old and a good student, I have a boyfriend, and the family is enjoying a break from tragedy. It's been a while since anyone has died, and the Sainte-Anne hospital seems to have forgotten our phone number. I'm studying at the Sciences Po, the ideal place to hone a slick and serious persona. I dress like most of the other female students, in navy blue, red, and forest green, Peter Pan collars and Levi's. I tie my hair with velvet ribbons bought by the yard at the drugstore, and wear fake pearls, with gold-plated hoops in my ears. I wear patent leather ballet flats and a plaid scarf purchased from an overpriced boutique on the Boulevard Raspail. I'm modeling myself after students I barely know who come from the Grand Bourgeois neighborhoods of the 6th, 8th, 16th, and 17th arrondissements, young people whose fathers are CEOs, who go to mass and attend rallies.

I try to bond with them though they look at me with suspicion when I tell them I'm not baptized. They never dare to question me outright about my origins, but they gossip behind my back about why my skin is so dark. By this time, my father has been nominated for a prestigious post in the Ministry of Culture, which has raised my family's status. His office is in a private mansion that the Republic offers to certain high officials of the state. There's a car and driver at his disposal, and he often comes to pick me up after school. My admiration for him knows no bounds. He's already written a number of books, some of which my classmates have read and praised.

I live in an attic apartment on the Avenue Bosquet, a tony neighborhood that I find depressing but which, at the time, I consider indispensable to my pursuit of the bourgeois life to which I aspire. As long as I live here, I figure, no one can suspect where I come from. I don't speak about you, about the drugs and alcohol or any of the folly and ruin of our family. I listen, observe, and learn. I'm a sponge. In addition to my courses, I commit turns of phrase and social mores to memory. My classmates are often blond and live in the grand apartments. They wear headbands and real gold jewelry. They hang out with boys whose outfits coordinate perfectly with their own. Some wear shiny signet rings on their pinkies. They play tennis, sail, and go on holiday together to their families' estates on the Côte des Basques in Biarritz or the Gulf of Morbihan in Brittany.

I copy their hairstyles, cutting my own long hair into a bob like everyone else on the Rue Saint-Guillaume. My mother observes my metamorphosis with bewilderment. Still, she's kind, saying only "It's not my taste but everything suits you."

Sometimes a tiny grain of sand enters this perfect bubble. One day I'm sitting in an amphitheater listening intently to a professor whose reputation for strictness forbids any disruption when a friend whispers in my ear. He tells me that a few days ago he overheard a conversation two other students were having about me. One had confessed that he thought I was pretty while the other found me too dark for his tastes. All these years later and the memory of these words still manages to have an effect on me.

My boyfriend doesn't come from this tribe. He lives outside Paris, in the suburbs. He's a brilliant Jewish leftist activist with long hair that he pulls back into a ponytail. Although his family background is unlike mine, we find a common refuge in the things that separate us from the others. We study for exams together, talk politics, and laugh a lot, squeezing into my little bed in the attic. We travel to places we've never seen before. One long weekend he takes me to Madrid. I don't know Spain at all except for the Costa Blanca holiday with the Georges. We go to the Prado museum, and to the Corrida. I don't like the blood and the brutality of this macabre ballet between man and bull but don't dare admit this to my boyfriend since the tickets are expensive, especially for a student. Instead, I choose to concentrate on the colors and costumes: the delicate embroidered silk, the reflections of the sequins, the glittering jewels, and the graceful movement of the fuchsia and saffron cape.

In the evening we choose a restaurant at random in the center of downtown. We splurge and order paella for two and a pitcher of red wine. As we sip from our glasses, my gaze happens upon a young man who's obviously agitated. Overwhelming fear seizes me—worse than fear, a panic as irrational as it is uncontrollable. The boy's strung out on drugs, I'm certain of it. I watch him go back and forth to the toilet with his friends. "We're in a neighborhood of junkies," I whisper to my boyfriend, who at first laughs off my worry. I break out in a cold sweat, drenching my light dress. Everything gets blurry as I'm overtaken by a wave of vertigo. The panic is so intense that my boyfriend suggests we return to the hotel. We leave a few bills on the table next to our meals, which we had barely touched.

In the days that follow, I keep an eye out, scrutinizing each passerby with suspicion and avoiding every public bathroom on the off chance I will run into someone shooting up. I will never go back to Madrid. You caught up with me, Maria, you with your syringe, your spoon and lighter, and the poison you consumed, which poisoned everyone close to you. After the relationship ends, that boyfriend and I remain friends, and he never mentions the panic attack that ruined our stay. Maybe he chalked the episode up to one of my many quirks. He probably doesn't even remember it anymore.

I'm about six or seven years old. We're still living in the low-income housing in the 13th arrondissement. My room, where I sleep in a navy blue metal bed, is the biggest. There's a large plastic desk—also navy blue—underneath the window. On the main wall hangs a giant handwoven Moroccan tapestry. To the right of my bed is a canvas tipi, where I've put a lamp, my dolls, a wooden crib, and a little table. I spend hours there talking to an imaginary family. Sometimes, I allow my little brother to take part in the game. When night comes, I pile so many stuffed animals on my bed there's barely any room left for my body. I don't know why I wake up that night. A cry, a premonition, the arm of a record player skipping on the last track? I get up and feel my way in the dark. An orange lamp that Maman leaves on all night lights up the hallway. I take a look toward my parents' room. They must be asleep since their door is closed. It's probably very late; there are only a couple of lights on in the neighboring buildings. I approach the glass doors that lead to the living room, still sleepy and groggy. And there you are, Maria. You had arrived the previous day just before dinner. Through the wavy glass, I make out your silhouette leaning forward, and I go to open the door. I don't know why I want to, maybe to prove to myself that everything is okay. Then I see the fabric tourniquet compressing your arm and your gaze focused on the needle as it enters your vein. Your head lolls to the side. You barely have the strength to pull the syringe full of blood out of your arm.

It's because of you that I have such a finely attuned radar for drug addicts. Every time someone stays in the bathroom for too long it sets me on edge. None of the dealers' gestures—the fake handshakes exchanged as the drugs pass from one hand to the other, the accelerated movement away after the drop happens—escape me. I spot every used and abandoned syringe and tourniquet, the blackened spoons and crumpled-up balls of aluminum foil abandoned in the gutter. For me, drugs are a captivating and panic-inducing magnet.

One Sunday, around 6:00 p.m. but already dark, a young man stands in front of me in line at a movie theater in the Latin Quarter. I'm sixteen or seventeen years old and he's probably only a couple of years older. He's with his parents, who watch him nervously. They seem utterly exhausted, so old already, much older than my parents. I don't say anything to them, but I can read the despair on their faces—the years of torment, the sleepless nights. The boy seems out of place. His skin has a yellowish tint and his teeth have already begun to rot. A gnawing unrest suddenly overtakes him. He says he can't wait any longer, he just can't. He has to go, immediately. Right now. His father takes him by the arms and pleads with him not to go, not to ruin this "family moment," to hold on just a little longer. His voice betrays an expectation of failure—the weariness of a scene that has played out a thousand times before, a battle that's already lost. He fervently grips the frail body of his son knowing full well where he'll go once he releases him.

I can so clearly imagine everything leading up to this moment. Going to see an old film in black-and-white at the art house, isn't that what good families do? They took this trip from their apartment to the movie theater dozens of times when their son was younger, all three of them leaving happy and talkative, sharing their impressions of the film as they hurried home to spend the rest of the weekend picking at Sunday leftovers before going to bed. They hope that bringing back this ritual will do him some good—remind him that life can be simple and enjoyable and make him forget for a moment all the suffering he's inflicted upon himself and everyone else. But too much has changed.

The young man tries to tear himself away from his father's desperate embrace. He asks for money, saying he's not going to make it. "I swear, I'm going to die if I don't. I can't hold on!" The mother and father search each other's eyes for a solution that doesn't exist. Their son asks again for money. No, he doesn't ask, he begs. The father looks straight ahead, his face full of resignation and shame, as his son searches his coat pockets. He lets the son find his wallet and remove a couple of bills and then watches him leave, turning the corner to who knows where in search of a fix. The mother slips her arm around her husband and huddles up against his black raincoat. She speaks softly, murmuring that there's nothing that can be done, that they aren't to blame. She reassures him. "He'll come back. He always comes back. We'll wait for him." I look at them holding each other in the cold and despair and think, *Yes, you'll wait for him.*

Like we waited for you.

I'm going to be twelve years old in a couple of days. It's 1981, an important year for us as well as for many other French people. The Left is poised to take power. At our home, the political gatherings multiply. Even though Papa has quit the militant Maoist organization, he continues to believe in the revolution. Five years ago, I saw him cry for the very first time in my life. I was coming home from school and found him sitting on a stool in the kitchen with tears streaming down his cheeks. My father—who had always been so strong, who carried the weight of our turbulent family on his shoulders—the person everyone went to when they had a problem, when his mother acted up at the nursing home, or when his sister called him hysterical after their brother committed suicide. I'd never seen him in such a state.

"What happened?" I asked haltingly.

"Mao is dead."

I remember sharing his pain. Chairman Mao was our model—the grandfather we never had. Copies of the *Little Red Book* were everywhere in the apartment. Posters of him looking proud and dignified were taped to the walls of the apartment and at the house in the country. His life story was read to me at bedtime. After liberating his people from tyranny he was going to do the same with all of the oppressed countries around the world. Of course now, in later years, Papa understands that the story was not as pretty as all that. Still, Mao's death was something. A member of the family had left us. A page had turned.

At the beginning of the eighties, Papa and a group of his friends prepare for François Mitterrand to come into power. Mitterrand is not Papa's ideal candidate—too conservative for his taste. He's not on the side of the workers, Papa says. He's there only to preserve the status quo. Still, my father thinks that with the Left in the Élysée Palace anything is possible, provided the revolutionaries manage to make inroads. He's been working hard with his friends in the French Democratic Confederation of Labor, whose first chapter he created in the Ministry of Finance. They imagine an economy where all the cars and appliances manufactured will last for decades and the market will be replaced by a more fair and egalitarian system; in which the workers themselves will manage the factories and equal wages will be introduced. Maman says she intends to vote for another presidential hopeful, Coluche, a comedian infamous for his vulgar irreverence. Papa doesn't want to hear it. He finds her choice "absolutely idiotic." They clash bitterly over the disagreement; it will be the worst argument of their marriage.

On the night of the victory, we're all in the apartment, dozens of people squeezed together on the wooden benches with the embroidered cushions. The men have long hair and beards, the women wear masses of tribal jewelry. There's a mess of food and glasses on the low table. Maman has prepared a cake, in anticipation, as though it's someone's birthday. There are African tambourines on the floor, flutes from Latin America, stringed instruments that I can't name but love to play with. My brother and I are the only children present. My mother, usually so strict with bedtimes, has made an exception for this historic moment. The adults drink wine and roll joints while waiting for the results. When 8:00 p.m. finally arrives it feels as though we've been squirming nervously in front of the television for hours. At last, the face of the victor, François Mitterrand, appears on the screen. The Left is in power at last! Cries erupt, tears of happiness flow. My parents take each other in their arms and dance. A champagne cork pops in the smoke-filled room. We aren't alone; there's a clamor that echoes throughout the housing project. We open the windows and wave our arms, signaling to strangers across the way. Everyone's happy. I remember a huge crowd of people, singing and chanting, firecrackers bursting, and Papa giving us turns on his shoulders to see over everyone's head. It's a euphoric night.

Returning to school the next day is less so. My best friend, Sophie, and I jump up and down as we hug each other. Sophie's parents are militant Socialists who voted for Paul Quilès, Mitterrand's rival on the Left, but at least we're on the same winning side. Not everyone is as happy as we are, and we quickly learn to hide our jubilation. There are some who talk of "the Reds" wanting to take everything away, and others who insist their families are getting visas to emigrate to the United States and Canada. I'm confused. It had never occurred to me that everyone would not share our joy at the dawning of this new era full of promise.

Papa soon becomes disillusioned. Shortly after the victory, he and a few of his friends decide to sequester his boss, the head of the economic forecasting department, in his office as an act of protest. According to Papa, he's "a bastard" who sold out to Giscard, making catastrophic forecasts for months on end to cast the leftist administration in a poor light. My father has a contact at the president's residence, a college classmate turned colleague, who was nominated secretary general in the administration. He calls him to crow about what they've done. "We've got him! We've taken over the ministry!" On the other end of the line his friend is infuriated. "Have you completely lost your mind? Let him go immediately! We are in power. We have a historic responsibility. The entire world is watching us!" The director is released and Papa returns home. The revolution is never spoken of again.

You don't care about the election of François Mitterrand. You probably didn't even vote for him. While publicly you embody excess and boundless freedom, privately you're quite the opposite. As is often the case with children raised with blurry boundaries, you fiercely defend the established order. You complain about the dirt on the streets, decry the student marches, defend the police, and advocate for strict application of the law. In 1968 you take part in a parade on the Champs-Élysées in support of General de Gaulle and against the "Chienlit" chaos of the leftists. Later, you will praise the right-wing mayor (and future president) Jacques Chirac. After your battle with drugs, your conservatism becomes even more pronounced. There's no one more severe in the judgment of others than those who once succumbed to addiction themselves.

When we have dinner with you, we avoid speaking about politics or your battle with addiction. We figure it's not our place to say anything, since in the end we weren't the ones to save you. None of us knew how to protect you, not your parents or mine, nor my aunts and uncles. Nothing we tried worked—not affection, advice, admonishments, threats, or even involuntary hospitalizations. Only one person was able to get through to you.

It's 1980 and you're in Brussels shooting a few scenes for a film. A group of film students are invited to visit the set. Among them is a young woman who can't take her eyes off you. She has the same long, dark, and curly hair you have. You notice her too, but you're leaving Belgium the next day. She makes a life-changing decision to join you, and she will stay by your side until your death.

A. immediately grasps that she must act quickly to preserve the new life she has chosen. You're in the worst phase of your addiction, shooting up morning and night. There's never enough, you always want more. You're suicidal and A. is terrified that you will die. She never leaves you by yourself. She chases away the dealers who hover around you and holds your hand in the ambulance when you overdose. Even when you scream at her to leave you alone, plead with her to just leave you in peace, she doesn't go. With all the energy of a woman in love, A. devises a plan. She doesn't know anything about drugs but swiftly learns all she can by consulting doctors and specialists. She researches the methods of withdrawal and decides the best option is to take you to Brazil, where it's more difficult to procure heroin and where (unlike in France at the time) it's possible to buy methadone, the drug that helps to wean you off the more addictive opiate.

You stay several months in Brazil. I imagine the two of you there, A. clinging to hope and you twisting in pain from the withdrawal, certain you're going to die. Then, little by little, calm sets in. Life begins again, and the small pleasures return. The warmth of the sun on your body, the shocking taste of tart, juicy fruit exploding in your mouth. Finally, after nearly a year, A. believes you're ready for a comeback—that you're finished with drugs and that, since you're still young, you can return to your career and convince the film world they can count on you. There will be relapses, each one more painful than the last, but in the years after Brazil your long story with heroin finally comes to an end. You replace the syringe with a dizzying quantity of weed and then red wine and cigarettes, always cigarettes. So many cigarettes.

No one knew, but you never cut ties with Brando. The two of you continued to write to one another on a regular basis. You tell me this in passing, as though it's a mundane detail. The shared trauma of those few weeks of filming had bonded you for life. Brando left France without commenting on the film. Years later he declared publicly, "*Last Tango in Paris* required a lot of emotional arm wrestling with myself, and when it was finished, I decided that I wasn't ever again going to destroy myself emotionally to make a movie." He would not speak of it again. The rest, it seems, he told only you.

The film shoot took place at one of the worst times in his life. His wife Anna had recently kidnapped their son, Christian, the same son who years later would sink into drug abuse and become infamous for shooting his little sister's young boyfriend. You tell me Brando felt Bertolucci's manipulation as keenly as you did. "We felt very uncomfortable, both of us, after seeing the film for the first time at the premiere," you tell *Paris Match* in an interview after his death in 2004. "Not so much by the physical scenes as by what we were saying. Bertolucci made us do improvisational work, having us recount memories from our childhoods. Marlon found it more shameful than the nudity. He felt betrayed." For years, Brando refused all contact with the

Italian director, responding to neither his calls nor his letters. After fifteen years of silence, he decided to turn the page. He invited Bertolucci to visit him in Los Angeles, where the two men discussed the film and hashed out their differences. Brando was obviously less resentful. He also had less to forgive.

Heroin is everywhere. Now it's your half sister Fiona's turn to be hospitalized. Your father is hooked too. The actor's large luxurious apartment is where everyone gathers to get wasted. In a photo that Fiona keeps like a trophy, she's sitting on her father's lap. He wears a striped sports coat over a white shirt, like the Godfather, and Fiona still has a fresh and open baby face. She beams triumphantly, sure that she's finally entered the circle of the sacred monsters. She's starring in Alexandre Arcady's *The Big Carnival* alongside Philippe Noiret. In the snapshot taken at the film's premiere party, father and daughter look down the lens of the camera. Fiona wears a dress with a black corset bustier. Just underneath the bustline there's a clearly visible outline of a white rectangle. It looks as though she simply forgot to remove a label. "It was a packet of heroin!" she confesses to me later, giggling like a child. A few years after this picture was taken, when she is admitted for her own stint at Sainte-Anne, one of the nurses remarks that you had once occupied the very same room.

For a long time, I was wary of actors. I was frightened by what I perceived to be their hollowness, their thin-skinned narcissism and self-destructiveness—their incredible fear of aging, and the highs and lows of their careers in a system that builds them up and then just as quickly forgets about them. The cruelty of living as an object of desire. "Actors are lost children," my friend Laure tells me. Like you, she found success early—by the time we met in high school at seventeen she had already received a César.

When asked why she chose to act, the actress Nicole Garcia responded, "To be seen in a way that was otherwise missing from my life." Perhaps you felt the same. If so, how could you, Maria, a child who grew up invisible to the very people whose affection you needed most—how could you have become anything but an actress?

On November 3, 1978, *Paris Match* publishes an article with a headline ten years too late. "Maria Schneider Found Her Father." A few months earlier they had been delighted to see you as an isolated drug addict lost in the Scandinavian countryside. Now they seem to have invented a reconciliation between father and daughter. Apparently, Maria Schneider still sells. The cover is devoted to the inauguration of John Paul II as pope. Inside, the issue also covers Sylvester Stallone, Serge Gainsbourg, and Jane Birkin. Further in there's a report on Patty Hearst, the kidnapped granddaughter of the billionaire publisher William Randolph Hearst, who famously converted to the cause of the terrorist group that abducted her. Patty's back in good standing now and about to marry the police officer who was assigned to protect her. Between an advertisement for the Betamax, the first video cassette player, and another for Vittel water, the style section celebrates "the return of the leg." "It's a "rediscovery of the sexiest part of the woman's body, hidden for so long under long skirts and boots."

You don't appear to understand that fashion trends have changed. In the pictures that accompany the article you wear your own vintage clothing. An un-ironed men's shirt, a dingy denim jacket, and a long skirt, with wooden clogs. Your hair is un-brushed. On the left of the page is a photo of you and your father posing together. Gélin, the consummate seducer, wears a wool turtleneck sweater. This time he's the one who appears unhappy. At the request of the weekly magazine, he's come to join you on the set of *A Woman Like Eve*, a film that will be forgotten soon after it premieres. He has his arm wrapped around your waist, clutching you as if to keep you from floating away. You're twenty-six years old but look much older—the heroin has begun to do its work. You look into the camera dazed, as if you're not really seeing it. In another photograph, Gélin wears an unbuttoned shirt revealing a hairless torso, on his right he embraces his new wife (who, the magazine points out, is the same age as you). You're on his left, and on the end, with her head tipped toward you, your half sister, Fiona, pouts.

I find that every time I try to stop thinking about you, you hook me again.

The magazine I work for sends me to New York to write about Patti Smith at the Hotel Chelsea, the mythical place where everything started for her in the seventies. The singer refuses to speak to me about the hotel. She's on tour and exhausted. She feels like she's already said it all in her memoir. Since she won't speak to me directly, I consume all of the published material I can. In an interview for her 2012 album *Banga*, I come across a mention of a song she wrote, a sweet and melancholy farewell with a guitar riff you would have adored. The song is called "Maria." Patti Smith apparently wrote it the day after your death. You met each other sometime in the mid-seventies in California, where you had gone in search of silence and the warmth of the desert, the hippie life, and the drugs.

I knew you, when we were young, Smith sings.

Our family never heard you mention Patti Smith. Perhaps you wanted to keep this meeting for yourself, or maybe you were less affected by the singer with the cavernous voice than she was by you. It's one of the many mysteries you took away with you.

The photo is dated October 19, 2002, Fiona's wedding day. Your father, with his white hair, matching scarf, and the smile of an eternal charmer, is sitting in a car, visibly exhausted after having just left the hospital to walk your sister down the aisle. He will die a month later. Beside him, on the sidewalk, your half sister stands, dressed in a white embroidered lace gown. She has you enveloped in her arms. You have the ghost of a smile on your face. I can discern a glimmer of anxiety in your expression as though you're asking yourself what you're doing there. To the left of the bride, your half brother stands on tiptoe in an effort to hold his own among all these women. On Fiona's right is their mother, Sylvie Hirsch, the former model, who has grown softer with the years. The groom isn't even in the photo. Unsurprisingly, he didn't last long.

You had run into Fiona on a subway platform not long before the wedding; it had been years since you'd last seen each other. She wouldn't let you go until she got your telephone number. From time to time, you would talk to me about her, saying she made you sad. You felt she was like you, but worse. At least you worked with the finest directors, you said, and acted with legendary performers, but she seemed hardly to have ever left the pages of *Playboy* magazine. Nevertheless, you felt a real tenderness for her. You shared the same father and many of the same torments. You also shared a cinema "godfather" in Alain Delon. Just as he got you the small part in the film *The Love Mates*, years later he got a part for Fiona in José Pinheiro's *Cop's Honor*, in which he starred. In 1985 she posed in his arms to promote the film on the cover of *Elle*. Fiona ended up on the same path that had ensnared you—drugs, alcohol, rehab. But this similarity never seems to bother her. On the contrary, following in your footsteps makes her proud.

For a long time I hesitated to contact Fiona. We had crossed paths only once or twice, at funerals, and I didn't know her very well. But in 2016 I find out from her press agent that she'd written a book in which you feature, and I propose a meeting with her.

Her apartment is in a nice area in the north of Paris, a neighborhood that yuppie couples are gentrifying at an astonishing rate. Destitute families are being forced out, and the local Arab grocers are being replaced by organic markets and vegan restaurants. The sidewalks are populated with overpriced strollers and bearded hipsters with oversize glasses.

Her apartment is on the ground floor, cluttered like yours with too many things. I bring her flowers, which she cheerfully tucks into a vase and places on a table. She offers me a cigarette and tea. Her voice is hoarse like yours—the voice of a woman who has smoked far too much and spent too many nights shouting over the speakers in nightclubs. She wants to catch up and tell me everything, to turn this reunion into some sort of party. She digs out photos of herself at various ages and spreads them all on the floor as though to prove to me that she was once desirable and desired. She shows me her 1983 cover of *Playboy* with the series of nudes of her taken by the actress Mireille Darc. I'm struck by how time has mistreated her—the years of excess now evident in her face, her faulty memory. She moans and laughs about the weight she's gained, and recounts stories about the men in her life. Like you, she's proud and speaks about projects that will probably never happen, refusing to admit that her career is most likely behind her. Also like you, she doesn't hide her health and money problems. She admits that she doesn't know what she would have done had her friend, the designer Daniel Hechter, not offered to pay the rent for the apartment.

On this particular day she's very excited because the television channel TF1 is going to do a story on her. I don't have the heart to warn her that this sort of channel is likely only interested in her fall from grace. She probably suspects it but is too seduced by the attention to care much about how she will be portrayed. The network has asked her to film herself, to help them capture her daily life. They ask her to use her cellphone, and have sent along a handheld tripod, which she finds baffling. There's something childlike about her—this fragile little woman who admits to having put some of her anger into her second book. It's not in bookstores yet, but she has made a point of sending it to TF1. She's proud of it and imagines it's going to bring her back to the pages of the magazines, make her a lot of money, and get her film and theater roles. The previous book sold very well, she assures me, though her brother and stepmother criticized her for misrepresenting some episodes of her life, and this bothers her.

"It's them who are wrong!" she insists.

I reassure her, telling her that memory is fragile and flawed, and above all, personal. Everyone remembers what they want to remember, or what they can after time. I add that the freedom to own one's personal narrative is an absolute right. I'm aware that I'm also speaking for myself, to assuage the guilt and malaise that I feel while writing about you. I'm bracing myself against the inevitable criticism I expect to receive, all the people who have their own relationship with you and won't recognize you in the portrait I've drawn.

Fiona doesn't want to let me leave. She dashes around her two-room apartment, wrenching open cupboards to find traces of your pasts. Eventually she unearths an enormous poster of you that she once tore from an advertising kiosk. She unrolls it, puts it on the floor, climbs on top of it, and assumes your pose—she asks me to photograph her like that. She mixes up names and dates. Her sentences are so jumbled that I have a hard time following the thread of her reminiscences—her father and mother, the hospitalizations, her friends, lovers, the roles and her antics, you, A., her brothers, and Corsica, Cannes, Paris, and Oléron. It all merges into one long, confusing monologue, and I begin to find the apartment oppressive. Taking advantage of the sun coming out on an otherwise rainy day, I propose a walk. She tells me she's hungry and knows a nice restaurant in the neighborhood. Out in the street she introduces me to the merchants she knows. I'm reassured to see that she knows people in her neighborhood. At the restaurant she orders several plates and consumes them with gusto. After we finish our lunch I'm seized by a profound fatigue. Fiona still wants to talk, but I can't go on. I'm spent. I hail a taxi instead of taking the Métro. As soon as I get home, I fall into my bed and sleep for three long hours.

You didn't have any children, nor did you ever seem particularly interested in them. When I speak about mine to you, I can tell you're only pretending to listen. You never wanted to be a mother. The only time I saw you with a child was on-screen in *Wanted: Babysitter*, the last film by René Clément, a banal and unsuccessful thriller that was released in 1975. In it you play Michelle, a young student in Rome who watches children during the day to make a living and is abducted along with the boy she's taking care of. In the first frame of the film, your beauty saturates the screen. I've never seen you look so elegant. Clément captures your smile and your luminescence when other directors fed only on your darkness. It's not your greatest film. It lacks the intensity of *The Passenger*, but it's the one that touches me the most. Overlying its improbable kidnapping plot is another, more significant story. Your character studies architecture while your roommate, Ann, played by Sydne Rome, is studying to be an actress. Ann gets a part in a film and soon finds herself in an unscripted sex scene of which she has not been forewarned. The director asks her to take off her clothes. She declines. "If you refuse this role, it's over. You can start your career at zero!" threatens Ann's fictional costar, played by Robert Vaughn. The two men—the director and the actor—join forces against Ann, and she leaves the set screaming, "It was not in the script!" The director shouts after her, "What do you take yourself for? You think you were hired for your mind?"

It's hard not to see this scene as a nod to what you endured all those years ago.

There are battered women, women whose lipstick has smeared onto their chins, women with mascara smudged underneath glazed eyes. Women laughing at their reflections in dirty mirrors. Women smoking, languishing on stained mattresses. Women in the shower, dancing women, women fucking, crying, masturbating. Women with round bellies, women marrying each other. Women who love women, women who love men. There are also men. Men who are pale as death, having sex on crumpled sheets. Men shooting heroin. Beautiful men whose teeth have decayed from the dope. Men drinking. Men doing ecstasy. Men sick with AIDS. Men pissing in dirty toilets. Men ejaculating, men laughing, melancholy men looking through fogged windows.

These are about seven hundred images taken by the photographer Nan Goldin between 1979 and 1986. Together they make up a journal in photos—the result of years of wandering between Berlin, Mexico, Boston, Paris, and New York, adventures broken up by rare and precious moments of calm. These are images from the street, from parties, hotel rooms, and bathrooms. The artist gathered the pictures together under the title *Ballad of Sexual Dependency*—because it is indeed dependence that links these photos as they parade across the screen to an intoxicating soundtrack of the Velvet Underground, Bizet's *Carmen*, Jimmy Somerville, and Screamin' Jay Hawkins. Dependence on sex, but also dependence on love and violence, alcohol and drugs, unhappiness and pleasure.

It's the winter of 2017, and the exposition is on display at the Museum of Modern Art in New York. In the first room, I sit down in the dark to watch the film. While Maria Callas sings *Love is a child of Bohème* between the images of damaged bodies and faces, a photo of you jumps out at me.

I doubt you would relish seeing your face in this gallery of lost souls.

In 2001, *Vogue* magazine hired Nan Goldin to do a series of portraits published under the name "Strip-Project." Of all the women she might have chosen, you were the one she most wanted. You, who for so long had refused all photo shoots, agreed to do this one after the first meeting and never regretted it. You're wearing a black silk blouse, your typical jeans, and a pair of long earrings. Your shiny dark hair tumbles to the middle of your back; it was never so long as it was during this period. An Andalusian fan rests on your lap. Jewel-toned curtains frame the sofa where you sit cross-legged with a straight back. The picture resembles a Renaissance painting. This is the photo of you Goldin has decided to include in *The Ballad of Sexual Dependency*.

After the *Vogue* shoot you and Nan became friends, and you dined together regularly. A. even took care of her studio for a while. I imagine the two of you discussing film, the taboo lives you both led in America, the effectiveness of methadone versus herbal remedies to get off heroin, bisexuality, the countless parties that gave your respective lives their rhythm. All those years you were in such close proximity to one another, moving in the same social circles, and yet you never met. Perhaps you also spoke about unhappy subjects, the dramas you endured in your parallel lives. The suicides of her sister and your brother, your mutual death dance on the high wire.

But no, it would not have been like you to brood on such things.

I'm a child and my uncle Jean comes by the house from time to time. He's the oldest of the brothers, twenty years older than Papa—a "real" Schneider. We call him "Jeannot." My grandmother adores him. Jeannot is openly gay when few men of his generation are. He has a habit of describing his sexual escapades in excruciating detail—the men he's picked up on the cruise ship where he works as a steward, or the men he's met at the opera. His first lover during the war was an occupying German and his second an American during the liberation. Jeannot tells so many stories that we suspect him of lying but at the same time wonder how he could possibly invent them all. When he's speaking, Maman and Papa are always on edge, uncertain what will come out of his mouth next. In these moments, they invariably find something urgent with which to occupy themselves, some chore that must be attended to immediately: coffee to retrieve in the kitchen, the rest of the dishes to wash. But there's no escaping Jeannot's stories; he follows my parents from room to room, never letting them slip away.

There's one story he finds particularly amusing and repeats as often as he can. "I slept with Brando twenty years before Maria did in *Tango!*" it begins. During the postwar years, he says, he left his family to make his fortune in America. He assured his siblings that the next time they saw him, his arms would be weighed down with gold. The adventure didn't turn out exactly as he had hoped. No one was waiting for Jeannot in New York except the men cruising the waterfront. It's there, he insists, that he met Brando. Brando wasn't an actor yet, and spent his time as Jeannot did, hanging out on the docks on the west side of Manhattan. Sometimes I wonder if he ever told you that story, Maria. He probably did. If he wanted to tell it, nothing would have spared you.

Jeannot has a booming voice that attracts too much attention in public. When he's at the house he's so loud that we're afraid the neighbors will hear him through the walls. Sometimes he leaves without warning and comes back half an hour later, triumphantly claiming to have just banged a guy in the public urinal at the local Métro station. He says it casually, as though he'd merely gone out to buy a baguette. One day it's too much for my father, and he loses his temper. He's not angry that Jeannot is talking about sex in front of us—our parents subscribe to the belief that nothing should be hidden from children, as the French pediatrician Françoise Dolto advises—Papa merely wishes Jeannot wouldn't seek sex in our neighborhood, where people know us! Jeannot comes to the house less and less after that and then eventually, not at all. Papa still calls him from time to time, and then more regularly once Jeannot descends into full-blown alcoholism. Each time, Papa hangs up with a sigh, at once furious and sad. "When will he stop all this craziness?"

I've been out of the house for a long time when my father

tells me that Jeannot has died. Apparently, he went down in the morning to drink pastis at a local bistro where he was a regular. One pastis and suddenly Jeannot dropped dead on the tile, barely a moment after swallowing the last sip. "One pastis. Just one!" the server swore to the emergency responder who interrogated him. He was found to have one hundred times the legal limit of alcohol in his blood. I explain to Papa that it's impossible for it to have been so high, that surely they must have made a mistake. Yet that was the amount the hospital certified. In our family we don't do things halfway—not even when we die.

During the last few years, you come often to "Romanian Christmas," a dinner invented by my father and Uncle George held alternately at our home or his. The meal is Romanian in name only since no one knows how to prepare dishes from a country we so rarely visit. It isn't really "Christmas" either, since it takes place at the end of January, when everyone can fit it easily into their schedules. But it's a way to signify that we're still a family, even if we get together only once a year. You prefer it when the dinner takes place at the Georges'. At Papa's house, you are never entirely at ease, even after copious amounts of red wine and champagne.

Although the cancer is not yet diagnosed, you've recently developed an intense urge to rebuild family ties and propose that we organize a dinner among the cousins. I'm in charge of the first one. The four of us gather around the table in my little apartment on the Rue Martel eating the homemade mushroom velouté I had prepared, which had given me a lot of trouble. We drink and laugh, and when it's time to leave we all promise to do it again soon. But then you get sick and the idea is abandoned.

In the months before your death you say the same thing over and over: "I must see my mother." Not "I would like to," but "I *must.*" You repeat it even though the prospect of actually following through plunges you into terrible anguish. Still, in spite of everything, you don't want to die without seeing her one last time. You keep pushing back your trip to Nice, where she lives, citing the lack of time, the fatigue caused by the treatments, the panic you experience on airplanes. When she lived in Tahiti, you never went to visit. "Twenty hours without cigarettes," you said, "can you imagine?" But Nice is a lot closer than Papeete and you're dying, so you finally make the trip. Brigitte pays your way since you can't afford the ticket. You're there for less than a week before returning to Paris. You never talk about what happened while you were there, but for days afterward you are dejected and withdrawn—like a sad child who has lain awake, waiting for their mother to cuddle them at bedtime before realizing, finally, that she will never come.

Maman calls to tell me that Jacques Rivette has died. She's very emotional. They had known each other at the *Cahiers du Cinéma*, back when she passed her spare time watching films. You and Rivette felt a deep tenderness for each other. You acted in a film of his, *Merry-Go-Round*. At that stage in your career, your reputation was so bad that the big film directors were reluctant to take the risk of working with you. It was therefore all the more extraordinary that Rivette chose you. You lobbied for the casting of the Warhol icon Joe Dallesandro and, through your influence, Maurice Garrel and even Frédéric Mitterrand ended up in the credits. The director made an effort to make you feel confident, and you never forgot the uncommon elegance of this gesture.

Rivette was present when, a couple of months before your death, you were awarded the insignia of Chevalier of the Order of Arts and Letters—one of the highest honors one can receive in France. The ceremony takes place in one of the reception rooms at the Ministry of Culture on the Rue de Valois—a vast rectangular room overlooking the garden of the Palais-Royal, with imposing chandeliers and blue and yellow drapes over delicate woodwork. You never cared much about prizes, but you find a particular satisfaction in this one. It's meaningful too for Frédéric Mitterrand, who in the years since that disconcerting encounter with you in the rain outside L'Olympic had become a minister of culture. He arranged for you to receive the award, hoping to finally make up for what he must have considered his shabby treatment of you.

You're very weak, and leave your apartment for the ceremony with great difficulty. Your hair has been cut short, and it is undyed. The shock of your white hair pained me the first time I saw it. You wear a light blue jacket and jeans over your emaciated body and just barely manage to remain standing to greet the procession of people who want to pay their compliments to you. During the ministers' speeches, you remain seated, suffering particularly from the crushing heat in the salon. In vain you try to get a little air with the help of a fan. You smile for photos and interact with mechanical gestures. At first you stick the medal onto the wrong side of your jacket, as though you don't entirely believe it belongs to you. But at last you have been recognized for your accomplishments in your chosen craft. You didn't go through life for nothing. Now, you can leave it.

Bertolucci finally apologizes but it's too late to matter since you're no longer around to hear it. He was interrogated by the Italian press the day after your death and finally offered a quasi confession. "Maria accused me of having stolen her youth, and today I ask myself if it isn't partly true. She was much too young to have been able to withstand the impact and the unpredictable and brutal success of the film." He could have stopped there, but he's not the sort of person to leave well enough alone. "Her death came too soon, before I could kiss her tenderly and tell her that I feel as close to her now as I did on day one, and ask for her forgiveness."

You wouldn't have wanted his excuses. Even less his kisses.

After *Tango*, you never saw Bertolucci again except for one time at a Japanese film festival. Having had no idea he was there, you stepped out of a screening and found yourself face-to-face with him. He seemed embarrassed. In jest, someone pretended to introduce you as though, with the years that had passed, you no longer recognized one another. Bertolucci attempted an awkward "hello."

You responded with the same line you uttered as Jeanne at the end of *Tango*, after killing Paul. "I don't know this man," you said before walking away.

You still follow me everywhere, Maria. Without fail the little coincidences of life drive me toward you.

At the end of October 2015, I'm having lunch at a Japanese restaurant in the 6th arrondissement. It's the kind of sophisticated restaurant that has simple décor and exorbitant prices. I'm just beginning a conversation with my tablemate when I see her—the gaunt figure with the long white hair. It's Patti Smith having lunch with her agent two tables down from me. She speaks in a low voice as she finishes her soup and picks at a few pieces of raw fish. As soon as I see her I'm unable to think of anything but going to talk to her. Her meal is nearly done and I'm afraid this woman for whom I have so many questions will leave before I have the chance to speak to her.

When her agent goes upstairs to the bathroom, I follow him like a groupie and wait by the door. When he comes out, I hastily introduce myself: I'm Maria Schneider's cousin, I heard the song, I'd just like to ask Patti Smith a couple of questions. He seems annoyed. It's a bad time, she's just arrived from London, she's tired and has to perform tomorrow. He'll see what he can do. Fifteen minutes later, I lift my head and she's standing there in front of me. I'm petrified. She extends her hand and I stand up to face her. She smiles through a curtain of white hair.

"Everything's in the song," she assures me but adds that your death shook her.

"Do you remember where you met?" I ask.

She responds with a rapidity that surprises me, as though I'd asked her about something that had happened just the day before. "It was in Los Angeles in 1973."

The next day on the stage at the Olympia, standing before fans who paid premium prices for their seats, Patti Smith reads a list of the dead. Your name resounds in the microphone. Maria Schneider. The crowd explodes with cheers and applause.

The scene from *Tango* is always in the periphery, waiting. Even in 2016 as I write about you, I see a photo while scrolling through my Twitter feed. The American version of *Elle* has rediscovered it. A few days ago the photographer David Hamilton took his own life after revelations about the abuse to which he allegedly subjected girls came to light. The first lady, Michelle Obama, has just made a scathing speech denouncing the demeaning, "hateful" language Donald Trump used about women during his election campaign. It's no longer necessary to be silent. Outspokenness has supplanted shame.

Elle has exhumed a video of Bertolucci at the Cinémathèque Française in Paris in 2013. The director is relaxed as he explains himself. "The scene with the butter was an idea that I had with Brando the morning of the filming." He confesses that he felt "horrible" about the way it made you feel, but still, he justifies the decision. "I wanted her to respond like a girl, not an actress." Regardless of the guilt he says he feels, he regrets nothing. "I wanted her to feel humiliated," he says. "To get something real, you have to be completely free. I didn't want Maria to play at the anger and humiliation, I wanted her to *feel* it. She hated me for the rest of her life for it."

Art before everything. To him, you were merely collateral

damage. It's what you'd been saying all along, but you may as well have been shouting into the void. No one wanted to hear it.

In 2013 not much was thought of the filmmaker's comment. When the interview resurfaces in 2016, it ignites the web. *The New Yorker* and *The Guardian* pick it up after *Elle*. Then *Vanity Fair* and the Spanish, Latin American, and Italian media. The hour has come to denounce the culprits and bring the 1970s, when abuse was tolerated under the guise of sexual liberation, to task. *Le Parisien* reprints the article from American *Elle*: "In *Last Tango in Paris*, Bertolucci and Brando planned the rape of Maria Schneider." The polemic spreads on Twitter, in all languages and on all continents. The American actress Jessica Chastain types a ferocious post: "To all the people that love this film—you're watching a nineteen-year-old get raped by a forty-eight-year-old man. The director planned her attack. I feel sick." It's retweeted tens of thousands of times.

Facing the onslaught, Bertolucci decides to end his silence, beginning with this disturbing sentence: "I would like for the last time to clear up a ridiculous misunderstanding regarding *Last Tango in Paris* which continues to be reported around the world." Not wanting to go back on his last remarks, he stitches a new version together. "Several years ago at the Cinémathèque Française someone asked me for details on the famous butter scene. I specified, but perhaps I was not clear, that I decided with Marlon Brando not to inform Maria that we would use butter. We wanted her spontaneous reaction to that improper use [of the butter]. That is where the misunderstanding lies. Somebody thought, and thinks, that Maria had not been informed about the violence on her. That is false!" He continues. "Maria knew everything because she had read the script, where it was all described. The only novelty was the idea of the butter. And that, as I learned many years later, offended Maria. Not the violence that she is subjected to in the scene, which was written in the screenplay."

He's lying, but you are no longer here to give your version.

The early decades of the twenty-first century will be a time of moral reckoning. The victims are heard, and aggressors are pilloried in the media. I see an article about the culture of rape in the film industry. To illustrate, there's the photo of Brando on your back while you fight to get away. From then on, Bertolucci will have trouble securing financing for his films. Until his death in 2018, he will continue to defend himself in order to preserve his image and films for posterity. But his career as he knew it is finished. You might have been satisfied to see him facing such public derision—this man who had so terrorized you and is still contradicting himself all these years later. Maybe you wouldn't even have bothered to comment, content to just smile, with that wry, knowing expression of yours.

I accompany you to your last television appearance. My daughter's father was the editor in chief of a cultural program on France 4, and he always dreamed of having you on their show. You let yourself be persuaded only because at the time you were an ambassador of contemporary Italian cinema and had a cause to promote. You arrive at the dressing room with A., already tense, and ask for a glass of red wine to relax. We promise not to leave you alone. You refuse to let the makeup artist apply her brushes to your face, telling her, "I do my own makeup." Taking a greasy black eye pencil out of your bag, you line your eyes. Next you produce a powder compact and mascara, and apply a slash of red to your lips. You turn toward us to verify that everything looks good, and I don't have the heart to tell you that you might have been better off had you accepted the services of a professional.

All day long you had worked to memorize the names of the Italian films you've come to speak about. On the set you clutch a little red pouch with the titles in it, like a schoolgirl with a cheat sheet. As usual, you're wearing jeans, a men's white shirt, and a three-quarter-length dark red coat. Your hair is very long, the disheveled bangs covering your forehead. The music blaring from the speakers seems to bother you. You adjust your earpiece and occasionally ask for a question to be repeated. The presenter feels your tension. He tries an old journalistic technique of flattering the ego of the recalcitrant artist in order to get them to respond to a particular question. He mentions the fifty films you have acted in. You coyly correct him: "Fifty-eight." Presumably, you're including the cameos. When the journalist mentions the film *The Repentant*, where you played a small role opposite Isabelle Adjani, you say, "It's not a very good film. It wasn't sincere. A crowd-pleaser."

You smile again when you tell him that it's the Italian films, and the neorealism in particular that made you want to be an actress. You cite *L'Avventura, Blow-Up, Red Desert.* The interviewer listens politely, but as always, it's clear that's not what he wants to hear. He tries to pull you back onto the *Tango* track. You pretend not to notice and evade the question so skillfully that he almost apologizes for asking. You finally respond, "This movie remains in film history but it's not my favorite. Brando felt bullied, violated, and abused. I did too. But he was fifty years old and I was twenty." On the subject of Bertolucci you say only "I don't forgive him."

By comparison, you touch on the directorial styles of two French directors, Jacques Rivette and Phillipe Garrel. "They don't objectify their actors," you say. Then, seamlessly, you bring the conversation back to why you are there. Rolling your *r*'s impeccably, you sing the names of a string of mythic Italian directors: Antonioni, Comencini, Zeffirelli, Moretti, Benigni, Tornatore. On this small set, in front of the France 4 cameras, you are performing again. In your throaty voice, you conjure the world of Italian cinema and bring it to life.

• • •

Peacetime in Paris was not released in France. I've never seen it, but I have some secondhand knowledge of it because for many weeks it occupied all conversation in our apartment. The film was made in 1981 by the Serbian director Predrag Golubović. It was presented at the twelfth annual Moscow International Film Festival that year and won a prize. You play the role of Elen, which you accepted on the condition that you would not be required to do a sex scene. I don't know much else about *Peacetime in Paris* except that Maman played a part in it. You had heard Maman speak about her dreams of being an actress and secured her a small role. She plays a hotel employee. After reading the script Maman was reminded of what she had been told by her own mother, a Haitian woman who was raised in the high society of Port-au-Prince and then acted in a few big Hollywood productions before the war. "If you want to make movies," her mother warned, "never accept the part of the maid, they're always reserved for black women." It's the first time that Maman allows herself to work since quitting her job to take care of us. She's not yet forty and her beauty is devastating.

The prospect of having an experience in film delights her. I'm ten years old when this film is made, and I have never seen my mother smile so much. She stays on set to help, even for scenes that she's not a part of. A photo in black-and-white shows her behind the hotel reception desk. She wears her own clothing, a boiled wool vest over a low-cut blouse, her hair styled in an Afro. The operator's headset around her neck is the only thing she's wearing that doesn't belong to her. Her slender fingers rest on the dark wood of the counter. You are on the other side of the counter staring at nothing, and your Serbian costar has his head down. No one is looking at the camera.

Years later I notice another familiar name at the end of the credits: Daniel Gélin. In this film that no one else remembers, you had tried to bring your family together.

The water is so cold that even with a tan, my face flushes scarlet. After an hour of walking, I'm there at last. The waterfall breaks on the cold stones and hardened silt, and the air around it is transformed into mist. I'm holding hands with my lifelong friend Marie, who has dragged me here to make a wish. We are in Tahquitz Canyon in the desert, a couple of hours outside of Los Angeles. For the fourth time in two years I'm in California. At first I saw little reason for these repeated trips other than work or the chance to spend time with Marie. But then, in the dry land-scape with its monumental stones and the rocky paths where we hike barefoot, I came to understand that I was looking for you.

This time, however, I'm here for the sole purpose of finishing this book. During my previous trips I noticed that I have an easier time writing about you in Los Angeles than in Paris. Here, I'm lulled by the sensation that I'm breathing the air you breathed, bathing in the same light. What happened in those three years when you found refuge here? Between film shoots and other adventures, where you met Patti Smith and Bob Dylan, and plunged headfirst into drugs in a futile attempt at escape. What else happened? Perhaps I need to accept that I will never truly know.

• • •

In the United States in 1973, the Senate opens an investigation into Watergate, the Supreme Court legalizes abortion, the Wounded Knee occupation in South Dakota protests Native Americans' living conditions and demands the recognition of their rights and their land. The Vietnam War comes to an end in chaos. In 1974, Richard Nixon resigns as president of the United States, and in 1975, Saigon falls into the hands of communists after the Americans retreat. A trade agreement is signed between the United States and the Soviet Union in 1972, and the trade union leader Jimmy Hoffa disappears in 1975, most likely assassinated by the Mafia. In my imagination, these events do not weigh on you. I see you in those long shirts you used to wear, the silver bracelets jangling on your wrists. I see you looking out at the sky here, which is almost always impossibly blue, so real and cinematic at the same time. I see you surrounded by artists and hippies who are searching passionately for the same spirituality that you crave. I see you crashing in the painted concrete houses in this city that is at first so hard to love—this sprawling metropolis where everyone gets from one place to another by car and pedestrians are eyed with suspicion. I hear the music around you, the guitar chords and folk ballads. I see you warming your hands over a campfire after the sun has gone down. I imagine you lounging on a beach, a good distance from the water that's too cold for your liking. I see you in motion, gliding from place to place, searching for those sensations that drew you here from the other end of the world. Here in this canyon, I lie sprawled across a large stone that I chose because it's cracked in two. I look out into the distance, beyond the desert—San Jacinto Peak haloed by the dust of the eternal snow. I've never felt so close to you.

It was your favorite film, even though your character doesn't appear until twenty-nine minutes in. It's a long time to wait for one of the starring roles, and it says a lot about the place of women in film at the time. The drugs haven't yet taken away the fullness of your cheeks or your childlike smile. In a half hour you'll appear onscreen, reading on a bench.

The film begins with the main character David Locke, played by Jack Nicholson, having just arrived in post-colonial Africa to film a documentary. In a shabby hotel, Nicholson's character makes a split decision to assume the identity of a man he's struck up a casual friendship with in the neighboring room, after the man unexpectedly dies of a heart attack. Unbeknownst to Locke, the person whose identity he's taken is an arms trafficker. A slow and sweaty thriller ensues in which the fake arms dealer is pursued by very real criminals.

Your respective characters meet in Barcelona and form an immediate attraction while wandering through a maze in a park chatting about the architect Antonio Gaudí. Your character doesn't get a backstory. You're there without being there, hovering over the film like a ghost. You're there only to meet the man and to follow him, no matter what.

Nicholson is fifteen years older than you and he's one of the most prized actors in Hollywood. After *Easy Rider* he filmed

Chinatown with Roman Polanski. In 1975, the year *The Passenger* was released, Nicholson will also triumph in *One Flew over the Cuckoo's Nest*. You respect him, but, as with Brando, his stardom doesn't intimidate you. The fame of others has no effect on you. Michelangelo Antonioni, who received the Palme d'Or at Cannes for *Blow-Up*, doesn't faze you any more than Bertolucci does. The one exception to this rule is your father, who enchanted you for a time, but even that didn't last long.

When you return to Europe from Los Angeles it's as if you've arrived from another planet, dazed by the heat and the heroin. You wander in the desert of Southern Spain on quaaludes that you swallow with beer, and hang out with others around a shared joint. The sparse and dry vegetation where Antonioni has chosen to shoot is familiar to you now. You're living life at your own pace, drinking in the sun. The languor of the film suits you well. Its tension comes through in the slow, unhurried pacing of the shots. In the movie, Nicholson's David Locke talks about lies and identity—about the universal desire to trade one's own life for another. In English, the film's title was changed from *Profession: Reporter* to *The Passenger*, which seems much more appropriate. Nicholson's character is passing from one life to another, and you are a passenger accompanying him on his journey. You help him to run away from his life, he helps you to run away from yours.

After you become sick, we get together from time to time at the Ruc, the renovated brasserie a couple of steps from the Louvre. It has the double advantage of not being too far from where you live and providing the kind of luxury you appreciate—red velvet couches, black lacquered tables, and gilding. You have your favorite spot, just to the left of the entrance with your back to the window on a soft banquette. You've always been well received by the staff here in the manner that stars, even fallen stars, are welcomed. But since the cancer, your presence creates an awkward dilemma for the restaurant, the kind of place that prides itself on creating an easy, luxurious ambience for its guests. Your hair has gone white, you're gaunt, cough too noisily, and occasionally choke on your food. You tell me that once, because of the lack of air in your amputated lungs, you vomited on your plate. In time you feel you're no longer welcome at the Ruc, nor at the other restaurants you had once frequented. The beautiful servers look at you with a mix of pity and annoyance. Healthy people don't like to be around sickness.

I don't like to be around sick people either. Quick deaths are more familiar to me than the agony of illness. Fortunately, there are photos. Maman's photos, whole rolls of film that she's taken of you since your very first steps, and I lose myself in them when I want to forget the gray pallor of your skin, your emaciation, the dreadful breath that escapes your throat. I don't like to hear you say that you're going to be okay when I know you're dying. I don't like the looks you get from people who correctly assume you won't be here for long. I don't like the cough that brings every conversation to an abrupt halt. I don't like that you lecture me about the harmful effect of smoking cigarettes even though I know you're right. To me the cigarettes are an integral part of you. I've associated the scent of nicotine and patchouli with you since I was a child, nestling my face in your hair.

Her voice takes me by surprise. I'm in Saint-Tropez, having lunch with Brigitte Bardot's husband, Bernard d'Ormale, working on a series of magazine articles. Of the six pieces that I've been commissioned to write, this one is devoted to the icon hidden away in the favored fishing port of the jet set. "Brigitte," as she's called here, can no longer be spotted in the village. Instead, she spends her time going back and forth between her two houses, which she has gradually transformed into a menagerie. She kept the vow she made to you in 1973 at her apartment on the Avenue Paul-Doumer—that she would never act again and would instead devote the rest of her life to saving animals. Now, she's in poor health and stays out of the public eye, preferring to be remembered as she was, wild and proud, walking around the old city barefoot. Her former beauty is an encumbrance; she refuses to impose her age on the admirers who continue to gather in front of her gate. Her husband is now her link to the outside world—her intermediary with the local authorities, her unofficial spokesperson, her protector. D'Ormale doesn't wish to play any role other than the one to which he is now assigned: that of Brigitte Bardot's last husband.

We're seated on the terrace of the Hôtel la Ponche facing the water. It's the hotel where Brigitte once sipped lemonade with Roger Vadim, the man who would become her first husband after making her a star in *And God Created Woman*. It's also where Brigitte spent her first night with her third husband, Gunter Sachs.

Bernard d'Ormale is not a jealous man. While not the most prestigious of her lovers, he has the satisfaction of having been with her the longest. He picks at a salad like a man who still thinks about his looks while he talks about "Brigitte" and "Saint-Tropez"—the barrage of letters she receives every day and the hours she spends responding to each one by hand on white stationery. He tells me about her health problems and the fight for animal rights, both of which he can tell exhaust her. His tone is soft as he frets about her. Toward the end of the meal, I mention your name and he's surprised by the family tie. He remembers the phone calls that Brigitte made to you every Sunday and how grief-stricken she was by your death. I work up the courage to say that I'd like to meet her, to tell her myself how much she meant to you. He repeats that she doesn't want to see anyone but that perhaps she'll speak to me on the phone. While he calls her on his cell phone, I focus on a poster for *And God Created Woman* that hangs on the ochre wall across from our table. After a couple of words he passes the phone to me.

Bardot's voice has retained the distinctive throaty timbre from her films. I hear your name in my ear as though it's coming from very far away. "Maria . . ." Bardot begins to reminisce as she slips back to the past in long, silken strides. "She was lost. I took her in like a little abandoned kitten and how she made me laugh!"

She tells me that she never saw you again after *Tango*.

"She wasn't lucky," she sighs. She pauses for a few moments, thinking, and then finally says, "Well, yes, she was lucky. She was lucky and unlucky at the same time."

She mentions that you called her again when you found out you were sick. I ask if she was surprised by the reappearance after such a long time. She was not.

"Friendship is like that," she says. "You can disappear from sight and then reconnect as though nothing happened."

She had offered to have you come visit her, but you didn't want to. You didn't want her to see you "like that." She understood. This is how the Sunday conversations began. I clumsily thank her for everything she did for you, and she responds with impatience.

"There's nothing to thank me for. It's normal."

"But not everyone would do it," I insist.

"I'm not everyone!"

Then she turns it around, asking, "And you? What did you do for her?"

"I tried to be there for her," I stammer. Even as I say this I'm overcome with shame. Was I? How can we ever really "be there" for someone who is dying?

The doctors authorize you to return home after the last treatments and before hospice care. From then on, you receive people only at home—you, the one who always wanted to go out, are confined to your apartment.

I come to see you at the Palais-Royal, where you and A. welcome me into the precariousness of your life. The apartment, even smaller than I remember, struggles to contain all the memories from the decades you and A. have spent together. You're too weak to get out of bed but you accept a few handpicked visitors with joy. Those who come arrive with bottles of champagne that you open immediately under A.'s disapproving eye. The other presents interest you less, with the exception of the meticulously packed gifts Brigitte sends you from Saint-Tropez. There's always champagne, of course, but also food. Bardot is determined to play her role, that of the attentive mother you never had, right up until the end.

During my last visit you are weaker than ever. You can't move around without leaning on A., who supports you by holding on to your waist. Even the simplest gestures are difficult and painful. Dependence has put you in a terrible mood. You grumble and curse. A. takes it, remaining ever faithful and devoted. I arrive in the middle of the afternoon. I haven't even removed my coat when you mention that Nan Goldin has just left. She cheered you up by giving you a camera, which you now present proudly to me, like a child showing off their latest toy. Your photographer friend assured you that it's easy to use and you want more than anything to try.

I lie down next to you on the bed. We sip champagne and talk about everything but the cancer. You instruct A. to take a photo of us and get annoyed when she doesn't take it fast enough, so you get up and try to take it yourself. We laugh at how using this simple device seems to be beyond our capabilities. Finally, we manage to take twenty pictures, silly snapshots of lightness, tipsy moments and laughter, moments that we don't have enough of together. I finally get out of your bed and kiss you goodbye. Another of your friends, the actress Andréa Ferréol, is taking her turn with a bottle of champagne in hand, and it's time for me to leave. "Only one at a time," orders A.

You've been gone a long time now. Over lunch with A., where we speak only of you, I ask what became of the photos we took with the camera Nan Goldin gave you. She tells me that she transferred them to her computer and that she'll find them to show me. I look forward to having them. Strangely, I don't have any other pictures of the two of us together. Time passes with no word. I assume A. has forgotten. She's consumed with grief, and I don't want to press her too hard. I finally receive an email with a file containing the pictures, but despite my many attempts, I never manage to open it. Perhaps our software is not compatible. At each of our subsequent meetings I ask A. if she happened to find a solution, some other way to send me the pictures. She never says "No" but vaguely insinuates it's going to be complicated—she doesn't know where to find them but she'll look for them when she has time. Without knowing the reason, I understand that moment will never come. Still, I implore her one last time. "I would really love to have the photos, even one or two if you could manage it. They are my last memory of Maria."

A. sighs. Finally, with tenderness she says: "You know, Vanessa, in fact, they were quite blurry."

About the Author and Translator

Vanessa Schneider is a French journalist and novelist. She lives in Paris, where she works at the prestigious daily newspaper *Le Monde*. For over ten years, she has written award-winning essays and novels that have been translated abroad. *My Cousin Maria Schneider* is her eighth book, and her first to be translated into English.

Molly Ringwald's writing has appeared in *The New Yorker*, *The New York Times*, *The Guardian*, *Esquire*, and *Vogue*, and she is the author of the bestselling novel-in-stories *When It Happens to You*. She previously translated *Lie with Me*, a novel by Philippe Besson.